## FREE Test Taking Tips Video/DVD Offer

To better serve you, we created videos covering test taking tips that we want to give you for FREE. **These videos cover world-class tips that will help you succeed on your test.**

We just ask that you send us feedback about this product. Please let us know what you thought about it—whether good, bad, or indifferent.

To get your **FREE videos**, you can use the QR code below or email freevideos@studyguideteam.com with "Free Videos" in the subject line and the following information in the body of the email:

   a. The title of your product

   b. Your product rating on a scale of 1-5, with 5 being the highest

   c. Your feedback about the product

If you have any questions or concerns, please don't hesitate to contact us at info@studyguideteam.com.

Thank you!

# CPFM Exam Prep 2025-2026
3 Practice Tests and Food Protection Manager Certification Study Guide [Includes Detailed Answer Explanations]

Lydia Morrison

Copyright © 2025 by TPB Publishing

All rights reserved. No part of this publication may be reproduced, distributed, or transmitted in any form or by any means, including photocopying, recording, or other electronic or mechanical methods, without the prior written permission of the publisher, except in the case of brief quotations embodied in critical reviews and certain other noncommercial uses permitted by copyright law.

Written and edited by TPB Publishing.

TPB Publishing is not associated with or endorsed by any official testing organization. TPB Publishing is a publisher of unofficial educational products. All test and organization names are trademarks of their respective owners. Content in this book is included for utilitarian purposes only and does not constitute an endorsement by TPB Publishing of any particular point of view.

Interested in buying more than 10 copies of our product? Contact us about bulk discounts:
bulkorders@studyguideteam.com

ISBN 13: 9781637756157

# Table of Contents

*Welcome* --- 1
   FREE Videos/DVD OFFER --- 1
*Quick Overview* --- 2
*Test-Taking Strategies* --- 3
*Bonus Content & Audiobook Access* --- 7
*Introduction to the CPFM Exam* --- 8
*Study Prep Plan for the CPFM Test* --- 10
*Principles of Food Safety* --- 12
   Food Protection Procedures --- 12
   Temperature --- 31
*Foodborne Illness* --- 34
*Food Safety Education* --- 45
*Facilities and Equipment* --- 49
*Integrated Pest Management* --- 58
*Food Safety Regulations* --- 62
*Practice Test #1* --- 70
*Answer Explanations #1* --- 82
*Practice Test #2* --- 91
*Answer Explanations #2* --- 104
*Practice Test #3* --- 113
*Answer Explanations #3* --- 126

# Welcome

Dear Reader,

Welcome to your new Test Prep Books study guide! We are pleased that you chose us to help you prepare for your exam. There are many study options to choose from, and we appreciate you choosing us. Studying can be a daunting task, but we have designed a smart, effective study guide to help prepare you for what lies ahead.

Whether you're a parent helping your child learn and grow, a high school student working hard to get into your dream college, or a nursing student studying for a complex exam, we want to help give you the tools you need to succeed. We hope this study guide gives you the skills and the confidence to thrive, and we can't thank you enough for allowing us to be part of your journey.

In an effort to continue to improve our products, we welcome feedback from our customers. We look forward to hearing from you. Suggestions, success stories, and criticisms can all be communicated by emailing us at info@studyguideteam.com.

Sincerely,
Test Prep Books Team

## *FREE Videos/DVD OFFER*

Doing well on your exam requires both knowing the test content and understanding how to use that knowledge to do well on the test. We offer completely FREE test taking tip videos. **These videos cover world-class tips that you can use to succeed on your test.**

To get your **FREE videos**, you can use the QR code below or email freevideos@studyguideteam.com with "Free Videos" in the subject line and the following information in the body of the email:

    a. The title of your product
    b. Your product rating on a scale of 1-5, with 5 being the highest
    c. Your feedback about the product

If you have any questions or concerns, please don't hesitate to contact us at info@studyguideteam.com.

# Quick Overview

As you draw closer to taking your exam, effective preparation becomes more and more important. Thankfully, you have this study guide to help you get ready. Use this guide to help keep your studying on track and refer to it often.

This study guide contains several key sections that will help you be successful on your exam. The guide contains tips for what you should do the night before and the day of the test. Also included are test-taking tips. Knowing the right information is not always enough. Many well-prepared test takers struggle with exams. These tips will help equip you to accurately read, assess, and answer test questions.

A large part of the guide is devoted to showing you what content to expect on the exam and to helping you better understand that content. In this guide are practice test questions so that you can see how well you have grasped the content. Then, answer explanations are provided so that you can understand why you missed certain questions.

Don't try to cram the night before you take your exam. This is not a wise strategy for a few reasons. First, your retention of the information will be low. Your time would be better used by reviewing information you already know rather than trying to learn a lot of new information. Second, you will likely become stressed as you try to gain a large amount of knowledge in a short amount of time. Third, you will be depriving yourself of sleep. So be sure to go to bed at a reasonable time the night before. Being well-rested helps you focus and remain calm.

Be sure to eat a substantial breakfast the morning of the exam. If you are taking the exam in the afternoon, be sure to have a good lunch as well. Being hungry is distracting and can make it difficult to focus. You have hopefully spent lots of time preparing for the exam. Don't let an empty stomach get in the way of success!

When travelling to the testing center, leave earlier than needed. That way, you have a buffer in case you experience any delays. This will help you remain calm and will keep you from missing your appointment time at the testing center.

Be sure to pace yourself during the exam. Don't try to rush through the exam. There is no need to risk performing poorly on the exam just so you can leave the testing center early. Allow yourself to use all of the allotted time if needed.

Remain positive while taking the exam even if you feel like you are performing poorly. Thinking about the content you should have mastered will not help you perform better on the exam.

Once the exam is complete, take some time to relax. Even if you feel that you need to take the exam again, you will be well served by some down time before you begin studying again. It's often easier to convince yourself to study if you know that it will come with a reward!

# Test-Taking Strategies

## 1. Predicting the Answer

When you feel confident in your preparation for a multiple-choice test, try predicting the answer before reading the answer choices. This is especially useful on questions that test objective factual knowledge. By predicting the answer before reading the available choices, you eliminate the possibility that you will be distracted or led astray by an incorrect answer choice. You will feel more confident in your selection if you read the question, predict the answer, and then find your prediction among the answer choices. After using this strategy, be sure to still read all of the answer choices carefully and completely. If you feel unprepared, you should not attempt to predict the answers. This would be a waste of time and an opportunity for your mind to wander in the wrong direction.

## 2. Reading the Whole Question

Too often, test takers scan a multiple-choice question, recognize a few familiar words, and immediately jump to the answer choices. Test authors are aware of this common impatience, and they will sometimes prey upon it. For instance, a test author might subtly turn the question into a negative, or he or she might redirect the focus of the question right at the end. The only way to avoid falling into these traps is to read the entirety of the question carefully before reading the answer choices.

## 3. Looking for Wrong Answers

Long and complicated multiple-choice questions can be intimidating. One way to simplify a difficult multiple-choice question is to eliminate all of the answer choices that are clearly wrong. In most sets of answers, there will be at least one selection that can be dismissed right away. If the test is administered on paper, the test taker could draw a line through it to indicate that it may be ignored; otherwise, the test taker will have to perform this operation mentally or on scratch paper. In either case, once the obviously incorrect answers have been eliminated, the remaining choices may be considered. Sometimes identifying the clearly wrong answers will give the test taker some information about the correct answer. For instance, if one of the remaining answer choices is a direct opposite of one of the eliminated answer choices, it may well be the correct answer. The opposite of obviously wrong is obviously right! Of course, this is not always the case. Some answers are obviously incorrect simply because they are irrelevant to the question being asked. Still, identifying and eliminating some incorrect answer choices is a good way to simplify a multiple-choice question.

## 4. Don't Overanalyze

Anxious test takers often overanalyze questions. When you are nervous, your brain will often run wild, causing you to make associations and discover clues that don't actually exist. If you feel that this may be a problem for you, do whatever you can to slow down during the test. Try taking a deep breath or counting to ten. As you read and consider the question, restrict yourself to the particular words used by the author. Avoid thought tangents about what the author *really* meant, or what he or she was *trying* to say. The only things that matter on a multiple-choice test are the words that are actually in the question. You must avoid reading too much into a multiple-choice question, or supposing that the writer meant something other than what he or she wrote.

## 5. No Need for Panic

It is wise to learn as many strategies as possible before taking a multiple-choice test, but it is likely that you will come across a few questions for which you simply don't know the answer. In this situation, avoid panicking. Because most multiple-choice tests include dozens of questions, the relative value of a single wrong answer is small. As much as possible, you should compartmentalize each question on a multiple-choice test. In other words, you should not allow your feelings about one question to affect your success on the others. When you find a question that you either don't understand or don't know how to answer, just take a deep breath and do your best. Read the entire question slowly and carefully. Try rephrasing the question a couple of different ways. Then, read all of the answer choices carefully. After eliminating obviously wrong answers, make a selection and move on to the next question.

## 6. Confusing Answer Choices

When working on a difficult multiple-choice question, there may be a tendency to focus on the answer choices that are the easiest to understand. Many people, whether consciously or not, gravitate to the answer choices that require the least concentration, knowledge, and memory. This is a mistake. When you come across an answer choice that is confusing, you should give it extra attention. A question might be confusing because you do not know the subject matter to which it refers. If this is the case, don't

eliminate the answer before you have affirmatively settled on another. When you come across an answer choice of this type, set it aside as you look at the remaining choices. If you can confidently assert that one of the other choices is correct, you can leave the confusing answer aside. Otherwise, you will need to take a moment to try to better understand the confusing answer choice. Rephrasing is one way to tease out the sense of a confusing answer choice.

## 7. Your First Instinct

Many people struggle with multiple-choice tests because they overthink the questions. If you have studied sufficiently for the test, you should be prepared to trust your first instinct once you have carefully and completely read the question and all of the answer choices. There is a great deal of research suggesting that the mind can come to the correct conclusion very quickly once it has obtained all of the relevant information. At times, it may seem to you as if your intuition is working faster even than your reasoning mind. This may in fact be true. The knowledge you obtain while studying may be retrieved from your subconscious before you have a chance to work out the associations that support it. Verify your instinct by working out the reasons that it should be trusted.

## 8. Key Words

Many test takers struggle with multiple-choice questions because they have poor reading comprehension skills. Quickly reading and understanding a multiple-choice question requires a mixture of skill and experience. To help with this, try jotting down a few key words and phrases on a piece of scrap paper. Doing this concentrates the process of reading and forces the mind to weigh the relative importance of the question's parts. In selecting words and phrases to write down, the test taker thinks about the question more deeply and carefully. This is especially true for multiple-choice questions that are preceded by a long prompt.

## 9. Subtle Negatives

One of the oldest tricks in the multiple-choice test writer's book is to subtly reverse the meaning of a question with a word like *not* or *except*. If you are not paying attention to each word in the question, you can easily be led astray by this trick. For instance, a common question format is, "Which of the following is...?" Obviously, if the question instead is, "Which of the following is not...?," then the answer will be quite different. Even worse, the test makers are aware of the potential for this mistake and will include one answer choice that would be correct if the question were not negated or reversed. A test taker who misses the reversal will find what he or she believes to be a correct answer and will be so confident that he or she will fail to reread the question and discover the original error. The only way to avoid this is to practice a wide variety of multiple-choice questions and to pay close attention to each and every word.

## 10. Reading Every Answer Choice

It may seem obvious, but you should always read every one of the answer choices! Too many test takers fall into the habit of scanning the question and assuming that they understand the question because they recognize a few key words. From there, they pick the first answer choice that answers the question they believe they have read. Test takers who read all of the answer choices might discover that one of the latter answer choices is actually *more* correct. Moreover, reading all of the answer choices can remind you of facts related to the question that can help you arrive at the correct answer. Sometimes, a misstatement or incorrect detail in one of the latter answer choices will trigger your memory of the subject and will enable you to find the right answer. Failing to read all of the answer choices is like not reading all of the items on a restaurant menu: you might miss out on the perfect choice.

## 11. Spot the Hedges

One of the keys to success on multiple-choice tests is paying close attention to every word. This is never truer than with words like *almost*, *most*, *some*, and *sometimes*. These words are called "hedges" because they indicate that a statement is not totally true or not true in every place and time. An absolute statement will contain no hedges, but in many subjects, the answers are not always straightforward or absolute. There are always exceptions to the rules in these subjects. For this reason,

you should favor those multiple-choice questions that contain hedging language. The presence of qualifying words indicates that the author is taking special care with his or her words, which is certainly important when composing the right answer. After all, there are many ways to be wrong, but there is only one way to be right! For this reason, it is wise to avoid answers that are absolute when taking a multiple-choice test. An absolute answer is one that says things are either all one way or all another. They often include words like *every*, *always*, *best*, and *never*. If you are taking a multiple-choice test in a subject that doesn't lend itself to absolute answers, be on your guard if you see any of these words.

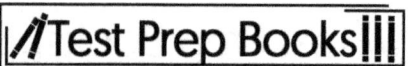

## 12. Long Answers

In many subject areas, the answers are not simple. As already mentioned, the right answer often requires hedges. Another common feature of the answers to a complex or subjective question are qualifying clauses, which are groups of words that subtly modify the meaning of the sentence. If the question or answer choice describes a rule to which there are exceptions or the subject matter is complicated, ambiguous, or confusing, the correct answer will require many words in order to be expressed clearly and accurately. In essence, you should not be deterred by answer choices that seem excessively long. Oftentimes, the author of the text will not be able to write the correct answer without offering some qualifications and modifications. Your job is to read the answer choices thoroughly and completely and to select the one that most accurately and precisely answers the question.

## 13. Restating to Understand

Sometimes, a question on a multiple-choice test is difficult not because of what it asks but because of how it is written. If this is the case, restate the question or answer choice in different words. This process serves a couple of important purposes. First, it forces you to concentrate on the core of the question. In order to rephrase the question accurately, you have to understand it well. Rephrasing the question will concentrate your mind on the key words and ideas. Second, it will present the information to your mind in a fresh way. This process may trigger your memory and render some useful scrap of information picked up while studying.

## 14. True Statements

Sometimes an answer choice will be true in itself, but it does not answer the question. This is one of the main reasons why it is essential to read the question carefully and completely before proceeding to the answer choices. Too often, test takers skip ahead to the answer choices and look for true statements. Having found one of these, they are content to select it without reference to the question above. The savvy test taker will always read the entire question before turning to the answer choices. Then, having settled on a correct answer choice, he or she will refer to the original question and ensure that the selected answer is relevant. The mistake of choosing a correct-but-irrelevant answer choice is especially common on questions related to specific pieces of objective knowledge.

## 15. No Patterns

One of the more dangerous ideas that circulates about multiple-choice tests is that the correct answers tend to fall into patterns. These erroneous ideas range from a belief that B and C are the most common right answers, to the idea that an unprepared test-taker should answer "A-B-A-C-A-D-A-B-A." It cannot be emphasized enough that pattern-seeking of this type is exactly the WRONG way to approach a multiple-choice test. To begin with, it is highly unlikely that the test maker will plot the correct answers according to some predetermined pattern. The questions are scrambled and delivered in a random order. Furthermore, even if the test maker was following a pattern in the assignation of correct answers, there is no reason why the test taker would know which pattern he or she was using. Any attempt to discern a pattern in the answer choices is a waste of time and a distraction from the real work of taking the test. A test taker would be much better served by extra preparation before the test than by reliance on a pattern in the answers.

# Bonus Content & Audiobook Access

We host multiple bonus items online, including the audiobook version of this study guide. Scan the QR code or go to this link to access this content:

**testprepbooks.com/bonus/cpfm**

If you have any issues, please email support@testprepbooks.com.

# Introduction to the CPFM Exam

## Function of the Test

The Certified Professional Food Managers (CPFM) examination, accredited by the American National Standards Institute (ANSI), is to be taken by those who work in food service. It is recognized by the Conference for Food Protection (CFP).

The test is designed for individuals who work in the grocery and convenience store industries. It evaluates the knowledge of food safety, proper food procedures, and other situations that individuals in these industries may face.

## Test Administration

Individuals wishing to take the exam can apply through Prometric. It is offered in three formats: in-person paper/pencil, in-person computer-based, and remote internet-based.

The CPFM certification awarded upon passing is valid for anywhere between 3 and 5 years depending on the test taker's jurisdiction.

## Test Format

The CPFM Exam consists of 80 questions in multiple-choice format and the total examination time for all questions is 2 hours. The content of the exam falls into six sections: Principles of Food Safety- Food Protection Procedures and Temperature, Foodborne Illness, Food Safety Education, Facilities and Equipment, Integrated Pest Management, and Food Safety Regulations.

| Section | Category | # of Qs | Percent of Exam |
|---|---|---|---|
| 1 | Principles of Food Safety | 34 | 42% |
| A | Food Protection Procedures | 27 | 80% |
| B | Temperature | 7 | 20% |
| 2 | Foodborne Illness | 18 | 23% |
| 3 | Food Safety Education | 8 | 10% |
| 4 | Facilities and Equipment | 11 | 14% |
| 5 | Integrated Pest Management | 6 | 7% |
| 6 | Food Safety Regulations | 3 | 4% |
| Total | | 80 | 100% |

## Scoring

The minimum passing score for the CPFM is 70% unless otherwise designated by the test taker's jurisdiction.

The test taker will receive an unofficial score report with a pass/fail notification after finishing the exam. If the score is passing, the individual will receive an official CPFM certificate with their test information a few weeks after taking the test.

# Study Prep Plan for the CPFM Test

**1** **Schedule** - Use one of our study schedules below or come up with one of your own.

**2** **Relax** - Test anxiety can hurt even the best students. There are many ways to reduce stress. Find the one that works best for you.

**3** **Execute** - Once you have a good plan in place, be sure to stick to it.

### One Week Study Schedule

|  |  |
| --- | --- |
| Day 1 | Principles of Food Safety |
| Day 2 | Temperature |
| Day 3 | Food Safety Education |
| Day 4 | Integrated Pest Management |
| Day 5 | Practice Test #1 |
| Day 6 | Practice Test #2 |
| Day 7 | Take Your Exam! |

### Two Week Study Schedule

|  |  |  |  |
| --- | --- | --- | --- |
| Day 1 | Principles of Food Safety | Day 8 | Employee Rights of Refusal |
| Day 2 | Manufacturer Instructions | Day 9 | Practice Test #1 |
| Day 3 | Temperature | Day 10 | Answer Explanations #1 |
| Day 4 | Self-Service Protection | Day 11 | Practice Test #2 |
| Day 5 | Food Safety Education | Day 12 | Answer Explanations #2 |
| Day 6 | Safe Food Flow | Day 13 | Practice Test #3 |
| Day 7 | Integrated Pest Management | Day 14 | Take Your Exam! |

**Build your own prep plan by visiting:**

testprepbooks.com/prep

As you study for your test, we'd like to take the opportunity to remind you that you are capable of great things! With the right tools and dedication, you truly can do anything you set your mind to. The fact that you are holding this book right now shows how committed you are. In case no one has told you lately, you've got this! Our intention behind including this coloring page is to give you the chance to take some time to engage your creative side when you need a little brain-break from studying. As a company, we want to encourage people like you to achieve their dreams by providing good quality study materials for the tests and certifications that improve careers and change lives. As individuals, many of us have taken such tests in our careers, and we know how challenging this process can be. While we can't come alongside you and cheer you on personally, we can offer you the space to recall your purpose, reconnect with your passion, and refresh your brain through an artistic practice. We wish you every success, and happy studying!

# Principles of Food Safety

## *Food Protection Procedures*

### Biological, Chemical and Physical Contaminants

Contamination of food with bacteria, viruses, parasites, or biological toxins (biological contamination), chemicals (chemical contamination), or other hazards—such as the physical hazards (physical contamination)—occurs when these contaminants are transferred to the food from its surroundings, from another food, or from a person, which may include employees or consumers. Here are some steps to avoid contamination.

- Receive food only from sources that obtain food from uncontaminated sources and that ensure protection from contamination during processing and transport—such as those on an approved source list or approved brands.

- Inspect food upon delivery to verify that it is delivered at an appropriate temperature (usually at or below 41 °F or at or above 135 °F) and does not appear to have been subjected to unsafe temperatures at any point before delivery.

- Store food in a dry, clean place, at least 6 inches off the floor, away from any chemicals. It should also be a location where it is protected from splashes (such as from water during hand washing or from chemicals), from dust and other debris, and from overhead drips (such as condensation from an air vent).

- Keep food enclosed in its original packaging or within another container or wrap.

- Separate foods that can cross-contaminate one another. For example, separate raw animal products from ready-to-eat (RTE) foods and unwashed fruits and vegetables. Also, separate different types of animal products from one another unless they are ingredients in the same recipe.

- Use different equipment and utensils—such as knives, cutting boards, and containers—for foods that may cross-contaminate one another. Alternatively, clean and sanitize these items between uses on different foods.

- Practice proper hand washing, glove use, and personal hygiene.

- Exclude sick employees from work when appropriate.

- Prevent contamination by consumers by, for example, providing individually packaged condiments, not re-serving uneaten bread or chips, and ensuring clean utensils are used for buffets.

Principles of Food Safety

Here are some examples of hazards that may be included in each of these three categories.

| Hazard | Examples |
|---|---|
| Biological hazards | <ul><li>Bacteria, viruses, and parasites</li><li>Toxins produced by these pathogens</li></ul> |
| Chemical hazards | <ul><li>Naturally occurring toxins, such as food allergens, mycotoxins, fish and shellfish toxins, and mushroom toxins</li><li>Chemicals from products like cleaning solutions, pesticides, and beauty products</li><li>Chemicals added to process or preserve food</li><li>Metals that leach into food from kitchen utensils and vessels</li></ul> |
| Physical hazards | <ul><li>Fragments of glass, jewelry, bone, or fingernails</li><li>Metal from cans or staples</li><li>Other small objects that could cause choking, cuts, or infection</li></ul> |

## Fish and Shellfish Toxins

Fish and shellfish can accumulate biological toxins, or poisons, from their environments and food, so their toxicity usually depends on their source of origin and feeding habits. Fish and shellfish toxins cannot be destroyed or inactivated by freezing or cooking, so certain types of fish from certain locations—including locations with temporary safety advisories—should be avoided by receiving fish only from safe sources that provide proper labeling. Unlike most fish toxins, Scromboid poisoning—a toxic level of histamine—develops after harvesting and can be prevented by maintaining fish under refrigeration beginning as soon as possible after catching or harvesting the fish.

Symptoms of fish and shellfish poisoning usually begin within a few minutes or a few hours of ingesting the toxin and resolve within a few hours or days, but some toxins can lead to long-term symptoms or death. Some symptoms are listed below.

- Nausea, vomiting, diarrhea, and abdominal pain
- Burning, numbness, or tingling sensations in or around the mouth, throat, or extremities
- Headache, dizziness, or a feeling of floating
- Joint or muscle pain, fatigue, or weakness
- Swelling, itching, rash, or dry throat and skin
- Difficulty walking, thinking, seeing, speaking, swallowing, or breathing
- Irregular heartbeat or low blood pressure
- Sweating; facial or upper body flushing
- Hot–cold inversion (hot food seems cold and vice versa)
- Paralysis, convulsions, seizures, or coma
- Tooth pain or metallic taste
- Pupil dilation

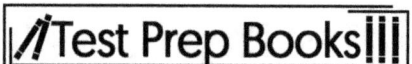

Principles of Food Safety

| Toxin | Common Sources | Additional Details |
|---|---|---|
| Histamine (Scromboid Poisoning) | Tuna, mahi-mahi, mackerel, bluefish, sardines, anchovies, marlin, bonito, skipjack, herring, marlin, amberjack | • Fish sometimes have an unusual appearance (honeycombed), smell, or taste (peppery, metallic, sharp, or salty). |
| Ciguatoxin | Barracuda, moray eel, grouper, snapper, sturgeon, sea bass, amberjack, mackerel, parrot fish, triggerfish, hogfish | • It can cause death.<br>• Barracuda and moray eel should be avoided. |
| Tetrodotoxin | Pufferfish (also known as fugu or blowfish) | • It can cause death.<br>• These fish should be avoided. |
| Shellfish Poisoning | Mussels, clams, oysters, scallops, whelks, and certain gastropods | • Paralytic shellfish poisoning is the most likely to occur and the most high-risk; death can occur in as little as 30 minutes.<br>• Neurotoxic shellfish poisoning is often associated with red tides and is usually not life-threatening.<br>• Diarrhetic shellfish poisoning is not life-threatening.<br>• Amnesic shellfish poisoning is rare, can cause short-term memory loss, and very rarely can cause death. |

## Cross-Contamination Prevention Methods

Cross-contamination occurs when potential sources of illness from one food (such as bacteria) pollute another food. The most common source of cross-contamination in a food service facility is raw meat. Handling another food product after touching raw meat—or using tools that sliced or chopped raw meat on another food product—risks contaminating the other food.

This can be prevented through good cleaning practices, including employees' personal hygiene in the workplace and consistent cleaning of equipment. In addition to knives and other handheld implements used to handle raw meat, any cutting boards and work surfaces must be cleaned with hot, soapy water before being used to handle another food product. Employees must wash their hands not only after handling raw meat, but also after handling its packaging due to the potential risk of bacteria. It's also important to remember to clean up before handling different types of meat. Because different meats are cooked at different temperatures, bacteria from one raw meat might survive and contaminate another raw meat that is cooked at a lower temperature.

The CPFM can reduce the risk of cross-contamination in their facility by enforcing cleaning procedures that make cleanliness a matter of routine. By creating routines, there is less need for employees to focus on remembering whether or not they're using clean tools and work stations. Routine acts as a protective factor. For example, if the CPFM requires employees to put all knives in a bin of dirty utensils after use in food preparation, it's unlikely that a knife used to slice raw meat will be used a second time and cross-contaminate other food.

## The Spread of Foodborne Illness

According to the Centers for Disease Control and Prevention (CDC), about one in six people become sick from foodborne illnesses each year in the United States, resulting in approximately 128,000 hospitalizations and about three thousand deaths yearly. Foodborne illnesses like *E. coli*, *Salmonella*, and botulism are caused by toxins or pathogens—disease-causing microorganisms—such as bacteria, viruses, parasites, and fungi. Each person involved in a product's journey from its source of origin—such as a farm—to the point where a consumer eats or drinks a product plays a role in ensuring that product is safe, including the consumers themselves. A **foodborne illness outbreak** occurs when two or more foodborne illness cases result from a common food source, and research shows that the majority of foodborne disease outbreaks have been linked to food service establishments. Food safety managers play a critical role in helping prevent foodborne illnesses, and this study guide explains key strategies that they can use to protect their customers.

Foodborne illnesses pose a greater risk for certain groups of people, called **highly susceptible populations (HSPs)**. These groups include preschool-aged children, people with a compromised immune system (such as from chemotherapy), elderly people, and people who eat food from certain institutions (such as day cares or nursing homes). Specific guidelines for these types of facilities help protect higher-risk groups from acquiring foodborne illnesses.

## Written Policies and Procedures

The function of a written policy or procedure is to provide employees with a readily available guideline for their duties. These policies are the foundational core of a facility's workplace culture, so long as they're used and enforced. A policy that isn't enforced, in essence, isn't actually a policy!

A written policy and procedure manual ought to be available in the workplace for easy reference by employees. This need not be immediately in the working environment, but should be in a space that is unlocked or made accessible during some portion of the day (such as the CPFM's office). Excerpts or abbreviated versions of relevant procedures may be posted in the workplace as needed for quick reference or reminders. This signage helps employees reference correct procedure when leaving their station is not practical (such as while in the middle of food preparation).

The Centers for Disease Control (CDC) recommend seven key areas a food service facility's policy should address:

- Roles and responsibilities
- Nutrition
- Behavioral design
- Facility efficiency
- Food safety
- Compliance
- Vendor reporting

However, these areas are a *guideline,* not a regulation. It is the CPFM's responsibility to ensure that the facility's written policies and procedures are appropriate to their particular facility insofar as the CPFM's authority and expertise allow.

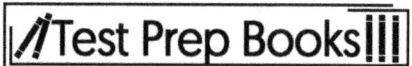

Principles of Food Safety

## Food Contamination by Employees

The personal hygiene of a food service facility's employees must be maintained to a high standard to avoid food contamination. In general, this prevents three major sources of foodborne illness:

- Allergens carried from outside
- Fecal matter or other pathogens
- Cross-contamination from other foods

In addition to posting appropriate handwashing procedures, the CPFM can reduce the risk of contamination by employees through developing and enforcing a dress code. Remember that the dress code's purpose is not to *look* a certain way, but to maintain a hygiene standard as a means of food preparation. Employees should keep their fingernails well-trimmed and cleaned, avoiding long or sharp fingernails, which might tear a glove during food preparation. Use of a hair net is required to cover all body hair, including any facial hair. Long hair ought to be tied up for ease of hair net use.

An employee's clothing and shoes should be clean, to reduce the risk of tracking dirt or other contaminants into the food service facility. Employees are expected to maintain daily bathing habits to ensure good hygiene. Unusual body odors are a potential sign that the employee needs a reminder about hygiene standards in food service.

## Personal Hygiene Practices

Food employees should also adhere to these personal hygiene practices, which are important to prevent contamination of food that can lead to foodborne illnesses.

- Wear clean clothes and bathe regularly.

- Wear hair restraints, such as hair nets, hats, and beard restraints.

- Avoid wearing jewelry on the hands or arms, except a plain ring.

- Keep fingernails smooth. Avoid fingernail polish and artificial nails unless covered by gloves.

- Securely cover any wounds or sores with discharge. If the lesion is on an exposed arm or hand, cover with an impermeable barrier and additionally—if on the hand or wrist—with a single-use glove.

- Avoid eating, drinking, and using tobacco products in food preparation areas.

- Food employees who have discharge from the eyes, mouth, or nose due to ongoing coughing, sneezing, or runny nose should be restricted.

## Hand Washing Station Requirements

Proper hand washing, a critical practice for preventing foodborne illness, involves washing the hands, exposed arms, and any prosthetic devices used for these areas at the right times and in the right way, as determined by current research. The following steps should be taken to wash these areas for a total of

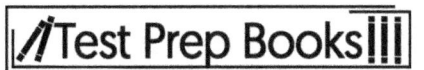

Principles of Food Safety

at least 20 seconds, after which a hand antiseptic that meets FDA guidelines can be applied and allowed to air-dry as an optional step.

- Use soap and warm, running water to wash in a dedicated hand washing sink (not one used for food preparation, washing food equipment, or other purposes, such as cleaning mops).
- Rinse, apply soap, and then vigorously rub these areas for 10 to 15 seconds, making sure to remove debris underneath fingernails and to include the fingertips and areas between fingers.
- Rinse off soap.
- Dry completely.
- Use a barrier such as a dry paper towel to turn off the faucet and open the bathroom door.

Always wash hands immediately before handling food or clean equipment that will be used with food, before putting on gloves to work with food, any time hands are soiled or could cause cross-contamination, and after the following:

- Visiting the restroom
- Handling raw food, if switching to handling ready-to-eat food
- Coughing, sneezing, or using a tissue
- Eating, drinking, or using tobacco products
- Touching body parts other than clean hands or arms, such as the face
- Touching animals, such as a personal service animal or aquatic animals used in a display
- Touching dirty equipment or utensils
- Using cleaning chemicals
- Leaving and returning to the food preparation area
- Handling anything that could cause contamination, such as money, trash, or cell phones

## Glove Usage

To prevent contamination, food employees should never handle ready-to-eat (RTE) food with bare hands except:

- When washing produce
- When the food will be sufficiently cooked again before being served
- When the facility has the appropriate permit and documentation required by the regulatory authority

Instead, single-use gloves or another utensil such as tongs, a serving spoon, or deli tissue should be used. To ensure that single-use gloves are effective for preventing contamination, it is important to:

- Wash hands first
- Choose the right size.
- Put them on properly (touching only the edge, not blowing into them or rolling them up)
- Change them when they become dirty or damaged, when switching tasks or types of food (such as after handling raw animal products, before handling ready-to-eat foods, or after an interruption to food preparation activities), or at least every four hours.

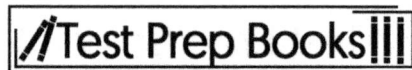

Principles of Food Safety

## Procedures for Handling Ready-To-Eat Foods

Any food that is provided by a food service facility completely prepared for consumption is considered a **ready-to-eat** (RTE) food. These foods do not need to be heated, mixed, or prepared by the customer in any other way in order to consume the food. Common examples include salads or sandwiches.

When handling RTE foods, the employee must follow all usual food protection policies to avoid contaminating the food. For example, following handwashing procedures, wearing gloves, maintaining personal hygiene, and so on are all required. To prevent contamination, RTE foods may not be handled with bare hands, even if the employee's hands have recently been washed or sanitized.

The greatest risk for contaminating RTE foods comes from storage. In particular, this applies to the storage of cold RTE foods such as cut fruit, salads, cold pasta, etc. RTE foods should always be stored on the top shelf of any storage unit. This avoids contamination of the food through the dripping of unprepared food onto the RTE food. RTE foods must always be covered and sealed when in storage, just like other food products.

The RTE foods being set out must be labeled. Often, it is wrapped in paper or another covering to reduce the risk of contamination. The required label indicates when the food was set out for customers and when it must be discarded. RTE food must be kept out of the temperature danger zone (41 °F to 135 °F) when stored to reduce the risk of bacteria growing. It may be kept outside those temperatures for limited time in self-service facilities (such as buffets). The length of time depends on the specific food and the means of temperature control, as described elsewhere.

## Thawing Procedures

Foods that are being marinated should be placed in the refrigerator. Food should also be thawed properly, not just taken out and placed on the counter. There are three different ways to properly thaw frozen food: the refrigerator, the microwave, or cold water. Thawing food in the refrigerator is a more time-consuming method. The time required to thaw food fully and safely is important to consider when choosing which method to use. Larger items take more time to thaw. The thawing time can also be affected by factors such as what temperature the fridge is set to and varied temperatures at different areas within the same fridge. After food is thawed, it is safe to stay in the fridge for additional time, depending on what the food is. Food can also be thawed in the microwave. When thawing food in the microwave, some parts of the food may begin to cook (but not fully), which makes it dangerous to hold and store. Because of this, when using the microwave to thaw food, it should be cooked immediately following thawing. The third safe method of thawing food is by submerging the food in cold water, though this should not be done in the three-compartment sink used to wash dishes. It must be sealed so that the bag it is in cannot leak, thereby preventing the food from collecting more bacteria. The water must be cold and stay cold, meaning that it must be checked and replaced around every thirty minutes. This process takes at least an hour, depending on the weight of the food. Once the food is thawed using this method, it also must be cooked immediately.

## Batch Cooking/Prepping Procedures

Batch cooking is the process of preparing and cooking quantities of a planned meal for a large group in multiple rounds of cooking. This practice is most common in food service for institutions that serve a single meal to all customers, such as schools. Batch cooking is preferable to cooking food once because food is at its highest quality shortly after it has been prepared. Holding food for the entire duration of an

Principles of Food Safety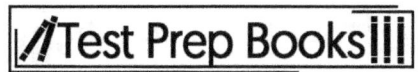

institutional lunch period reduces the quality of food for the final customers. Batch cooking also improves food safety because the longer food is held, the greater the risk of bacterial growth. Even if the food is held correctly, this risk is still present.

When overseeing a facility that utilizes batch cooking, the CPFM should ensure that all supplies are organized and sorted for use in each batch of food. Prepping the workplace prior to cooking the first batch often makes meal service more consistent by reducing the need to complete preparations multiple times. If the size of a batch needs to be adjusted, appropriate food supplies can be added when that batch is cooked.

As each batch of food is served, the facility should be preparing the next batch. This ensures that the food's color, texture, and nutritional quality is at its best when each new group of customers comes to receive food. The quality of food is especially important when the facility is serving an institution, in order to remain in compliance with local and federal requirements for institutional nutrition. Food held at high temperatures for a long time may be safe to eat, but it may also have reduced nutritional value due to the temperature breaking down vitamins and proteins and reducing other nutritional benefits.

However, not all foods ought to be batch cooked. If a food can be held for long periods without a reduction in quality or safety, it is appropriate to forego batch cooking. Likewise, some foods are complex enough that batch cooking is not a viable food preparation method. In both cases, the CPFM must ensure through training that their employees are prepared to make this decision based on the facility's menu.

## Cooling and Reheating Procedures

Rapid cooling and reheating of food is an important measure in food protection because it reduces the growth and spread of bacteria, which can cause foodborne illness.

Cooked food that is being cooled must reach the following temperature thresholds within the specified time allotted:

- Down to 70 °F within two hours of cooking
- Down to 41 °F within an additional four hours

A clean food thermometer should be used to ensure that these temperatures are reached internally. If possible, it is desirable to cool food more quickly. Reducing the temperature of food to 40 °F or below removes it from the danger zone. Cold foods (such as a salad) must be reduced to 41 °F or below within four hours of preparation.

Appropriate ways to cool food include wide, shallow basins; an ice bath; or leaving the food uncovered in a refrigerator. If the food is left uncovered in a refrigerator or in the kitchen, there must be no danger of contamination from food or supplies placed above it.

Food that will be served hot must be reheated within two hours of being removed from refrigeration. It must be reheated to an internal temperature of 165 °F. This temperature must be maintained for at least 15 seconds to ensure that any bacteria in the food are killed.

The specific requirements for cooling and reheating food in each state are listed in that state's food code. It is the CPFM's duty to be familiar with their local food code and to remain in compliance.

## Microwave Use

When a microwave oven is used to reheat food, the food should be reheated in multiple stages. Between rounds in the microwave, the food ought to be stirred or repositioned on the plate. This ensures that the food is reheated evenly. Even reheating reduces the risk of disease and improves customer satisfaction by avoiding cold spots in the food.

A microwave oven typically penetrates food by around one or one and a half inches. Thus, some dense or large foods may not be cooked or reheated appropriately in a microwave oven. The CPFM should consult their appliance's manual for directions about the microwave oven's efficacy. Some foods will come to a fully cooked temperature during the **standing time.** This is a period after the microwave oven has finished cooking during which the food is still heated by the microwave oven. This occurs because the microwave operates by making the food's molecules vibrate rapidly, generating heat. When the microwave stops, the vibrations continue to generate heat for a few minutes.

Always be sure to check the internal temperature of food cooked in the microwave oven using a clean food thermometer. This is especially important for thick and dense foods, which the microwave oven may not be able to heat as uniformly as a conventional oven. The minimum internal temperature required for food cooked with a microwave oven varies:

- Fish, beef, pork, lamb, veal, steaks, roasts, etc.: 145 °F
- Ground meats, eggs, and dishes containing eggs: 160 °F
- Poultry: 165 °F

These temperatures vary because each different food—and sometimes each different manner of food preparation for the same type of meat, such as ground beef vs. steak—provides a different environment that favors different types of bacteria. Making sure these temperatures are met reduces the risk that bacteria has survived and will harm the consumer.

## Time as a Food Safety Control

Using time alone as a control factor, TCS foods can be held without temperature control if consumed or discarded within:

- 4 hours after being removed from refrigeration at or below 41 °F or from cooking at or above 135 °F, with a label or other indicator of the end of the 4-hour period
- 4 hours if the food is at or below 70 °F when it becomes a TCS food—such as when a melon is cut or a canned good is opened—and remains at or below 70 °F for the duration of the 4 hours, with a label or other indicator of the end of the 4-hour period
- 6 hours for refrigerated foods that start out at or below 41 °F and are held at or below 70 °F during the 6 hours, with a label or other indicator denoting both the beginning and the end of the 6-hour period

Different foods have varied amounts of time that they can be held in the refrigerator or freezer before being discarded. Proper handling of food helps ensure that foods are not kept beyond a safe time frame, though it is important to know the safe time frames that foods have to avoid illness. Fresh lamb, veal, beef, and pork can be stored for different lengths of time depending on the cut of the meat. If it is ground meat or stew meat, it can be frozen for three to four months or refrigerated for one to two days. Steaks, roasts, and chops can be frozen for four to twelve months or stored in the refrigerator for three

# Principles of Food Safety

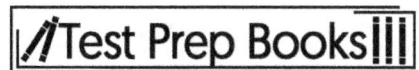

to five days. Corned beef can be refrigerated for five to seven days when stored with its pickling liquid or frozen after being drained for up to one month. Additionally, bacon can be stored in the refrigerator for up to seven days or frozen for one month. Poultry also has various safe storage times based on the cut of the meat. Whole fresh poultry can be refrigerated for one to two days or frozen for up to one year. If the fresh poultry is cut, it can be frozen for up to nine months or stored in the refrigerator for one to two days. Fresh ground poultry can be frozen for three to four months or refrigerated for one to two days. Precooked ham, if fully cooked, can be stored in the refrigerator for seven days if it is whole, for three to five days if it is halved, or for three to four days if it is sliced. Each of these cuts of fully cooked ham can be frozen for one to two months.

Fresh eggs in their shells can be stored in the refrigerator for three to five weeks but should not be frozen. The fresh yolks and whites of an egg can be refrigerated for two to four days or frozen for up to one year. Egg substitutes and pasteurized egg liquids can be refrigerated for ten days if they are not opened, or three days once they are opened. If they're not opened, they can be frozen for up to one year; if their container is opened, they should not be frozen.

Seafood, both fresh shellfish and fresh fish, can be stored in the refrigerator for one to two days; however, shellfish and fish differ in their freezing times. Fresh fish can be frozen for three to eight months, whereas fresh shellfish can be frozen for three months or up to one year.

Lunch meat, if deli-sliced, can be stored in the refrigerator for three to five days or frozen for one to two months. Hot dogs, unopened, can be stored in the fridge for two weeks or in the freezer for one to two months. Opened hot dogs can be refrigerated for one week or stored in the freezer for one to two months. Vacuum-packed sliced lunch meats can be stored in the freezer for one to two months, opened or unopened, and can be refrigerated for three to five days opened or two weeks unopened.

Raw sausage can be frozen for one to two months or stored in the refrigerator for one to two days. Hard sausages (such as pepperoni) can be stored in the refrigerator for two to three weeks or frozen for one to two months. Similar to the previously mentioned sausages, smoked sausages and summer sausages can both be frozen for one to two months. Smoked sausages can be refrigerated for seven days, and summer sausages can be refrigerated for three weeks opened or for three months when unopened.

## Potentially Hazardous Foods

Fruits and vegetables should be rinsed before handling. Raw foods, such as meat, should not be rinsed as this can cause bacteria to spread through water onto other surfaces. Raw foods should be kept separately from other foods to prevent cross-contamination. This applies to food being stored and cut since raw foods should be cut on a separate cutting board. Also, marinades should not be reused unless they were first brought to a boil. Food must be stored and cooked properly. Food should be cooked to its minimum internal temperature for safety. In terms of storage, it is important to properly handle food from the moment that a shipment is received. There is a temperature danger zone for certain foods (from 41 °F to 135 °F) which allows for the growth of bacteria. Foods that should avoid being kept in the temperature danger zone are time-temperature control for safety (TCS). Some foods that are TCS include poultry, dairy products, sprouts, and sprout seeds. Once a shipment of food is received, the foods should be carefully examined. The temperatures of TCS foods and frozen foods are particularly important to check. If TCS foods are determined to be safe, they should be quickly stored. Frozen foods should be frozen when they arrive. One sign that a food has thawed is that ice crystals have formed on the food's packaging.

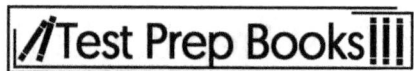

Principles of Food Safety

## Food Storage Placement

Foods should be stored in appropriate areas and at appropriate temperatures to maintain freshness. Dry goods should be stored in areas free of moisture, pests, and other contaminates. Goods should be stored at least 6 inches off the floor and away from walls. Containers should be sealable, airtight, and should protect the items from fluids. Chemicals, such as cleaning products, must always be stored in appropriate, airtight containers, and should never be stored near food items. Additionally, food should never be stored in non-food-specific areas such as locker rooms, mechanical rooms, under stairwells, or in restrooms or garbage collection areas.

TCS foods should be stored at a temperature of 41 °F or cooler. Frozen foods should be stored at a temperature low enough to keep them frozen solid. Raw meats and seafood should be wrapped or covered and stored away from produce and ready-to-eat foods to avoid cross-contamination. If separate containers or coolers are not available, raw produce and ready-to-eat foods can be stored on higher shelves in the cooler to prevent any drips from the meats from contaminating them. Refrigerated foods should be stored in a particular order if they all share the same cooling unit. Produce and ready-to-eat foods should be on the top shelves. Beneath those should be seafoods, followed by whole cuts of pork and/or beef. Ground meats and fish should be below that, and ground poultry should be on the bottom shelves.

Certain best practices should be in place to ensure that coolers and freezers are in optimum working condition. There should be at least one thermometer or thermostat in each unit to confirm adequate temperatures are being maintained. Coolers and freezers should not be overloaded, as this can restrict airflow and cause the unit to have to work harder and be less efficient at maintaining an adequate temperature. Similarly, shelves should be open wire shelves free of any type of liner or covering to allow for proper air flow. Food items should be randomly spot-checked to ensure that sufficient temperatures are being maintained.

## First-In, First Out (FIFO)

Food items should be rotated to maintain quality and freshness, as well as to prevent spoilage and waste. Foods with the earliest use-by or discard by date should be used first, before their expiration dates. Foods with later expiration dates can be stored behind foods with upcoming expiration dates so the new foods can be rotated in as older supplies are used. This is referred to as the first-in, first-out (FIFO) method. Foods that are received first are used first, and foods received later are used after earlier stock is consumed. Once the expiration date arrives, unused foods should be disposed of, and newer stock should be moved forward.

## Manufacturer Instructions

All appliances or other tools and devices used in the food service facility must be used in accordance with the manufacturer's instructions. The instruction packet, warranty information, and other paperwork that came with the appliance must be kept on record for reference as needed. Employees who will use the appliance must be trained to do so in accordance with the instruction packet.

Of particular note is the need for caution in facilities that commercially prepare food for distribution elsewhere. The use of **modified atmosphere packaging** (MAP) in the food industry improves the shelf life of packaged products, but also introduces new risks to both the food and the facility's employees. MAP utilizes gases to create an environment within the food packaging that inhibits the growth of

Principles of Food Safety

bacteria. Most bacteria require oxygen to flourish; consequently, increasing the carbon dioxide or nitrogen in a package's air makes it more difficult for bacteria to spread and for the food to go bad or cause illness. However, incorrect use of MAP appliances risks exposing employees to an unsafe volume of these gases or creating a toxic environment within the packaging. The symptoms of overexposure to carbon dioxide or nitrogen primarily include lightheadedness and difficulty breathing and can result in eventual suffocation. Prompt removal from the presence of these gases helps the employee's breathing return to normal.

## Types of Thermometers

Thermometers are necessary to ensure foods are adequately cooked, as research has shown that the appearance of food is an unreliable indicator of its temperature or safety.

| Thermometer | Usage |
|---|---|
| Thermocouple or thermistor thermometer | <ul><li>Quick, digital display</li><li>Sensor located in the tip of the probe</li><li>Can be used for foods of any thickness</li><li>Oven cord thermistor thermometers can be left in food during cooking</li></ul> |
| Bimetallic stemmed thermometer | <ul><li>Dial display; reading may take up to 2 minutes</li><li>Insert up to the dimple, usually 2–3 inches</li><li>Instant-read types can be used on thin foods by inserting sideways</li><li>Can be left in food during cooking, except for instant-read types</li></ul> |
| Infrared thermometer | <ul><li>Measures surface temperatures</li></ul> |
| Maximum registering thermometer | <ul><li>Displays the maximum temperature measured while being used</li></ul> |
| Time–temperature indicator (TTI) | <ul><li>Changes colors to indicate time–temperature abuse</li></ul> |

## Thermometer Accuracy/Calibration

Food thermometers must be accurate to within +/−1 °C or, if there is no Celsius scale on the thermometer, to within +/−2 °F and should be calibrated on a regular basis as well as after an impact or a drastic temperature change, such as using with ice water or boiling water.

## Thermometer Use

Correct thermometer use includes the following:

- Clean, sanitize, and air-dry thermometers before and after each use.
- Insert the entire sensing area—from ¼ inch to 3 inches, depending on the type of thermometer. The stem may need to be inserted sideways for thin foods like chicken strips, pork chops, and hamburger patties.
- Place the thermometer in the center or thickest part of most foods, such as casseroles, roasts, and individual cuts of meat or parts of poultry, avoiding bone and fat.

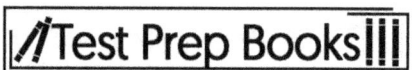

Principles of Food Safety

- Take temperature readings from multiple locations, particularly in whole poultry, foods that are not uniformly shaped, and combination dishes containing eggs, ground meat, or poultry.
- Avoid glass thermometers unless they have a shatterproof casing.

## Security

Maintaining appropriate security at the food service facility is required to reduce risk of contamination by non-employees. This is especially important for industrial facilities that prepare and distribute food through a wide area. Although the risk is low, deliberate contamination of food can occur and may constitute an act of terrorism. Simple safeguards such as security cameras, locked doors, and identification badges make it more difficult for non-employees to enter the facility.

Annual training about security requirements also reduces risk. In particular, encouraging employees to keep a "see something, say something" frame of mind improves security, safety, and product quality in all elements of food service. The goal of annual training is to provide updates on new policies or potential risks, and to refresh employees on why the facility's security matters.

In very large facilities or facilities that do not operate at all hours, it is appropriate to hire security personnel to monitor the building. The goal of security personnel is to make sure unapproved persons do not enter the shut-down facility or tamper with the exterior (such as power or water connections). This includes employees who attempt to enter outside of usual working hours.

## Admission Procedures

The food service facility's security is most directly supported through rigorous procedures that dictate who has access to non-public areas of the facility and awareness of what materials are able to enter.

Best practices for admission controls require minimizing the number of keys, identification cards, and other access tools that are created and distributed. In particular, master keys that are effective throughout the entire facility should not be held by employees. A typical employee should only have keys that allow access to areas required for their routine job duties (such as access to a janitorial closet for cleaning chemicals). Securing doors and entries also extends to freight doors and other shipping areas. Despite such a door's weight acting as a deterrent to entry, the CPFM must ensure that it is always closed and locked when not in use. Establishing a daily routine of checking that entrances are locked is an important procedure for security personnel.

The use of staff lockers with locks provided by the facility allows the CPFM, if warranted, to inspect personal belongings stored on site by employees. However, the CPFM must ensure that such an inspection is legal in their jurisdiction before proceeding. An inspection of personal belongings should only occur if there is substantial risk that an employee has intentionally brought harmful substances or objects into the facility.

## Delivery Driver Verification

For the sake of food safety, the CPFM should make sure that their facility's employees always confirm the identity of drivers and the accuracy of deliveries made to the facility. This requires confirming the driver's identity and that they work for the company that is providing the delivery. Even if a delivery driver is known to the employees receiving the shipment, their identity and credentials should be

## Principles of Food Safety

confirmed as a matter of routine. This reduces risk in case a former delivery driver acts with intent to harm others.

The food service facility should only accept deliveries that are delivered on the scheduled day or at the scheduled time, by verified drivers and organizations. Good communication with the supplier and the driver helps the facility track the location of shipped food products. This precaution helps make sure that the delivered shipment is the correct order and that the arrival is not a counterfeit delivery. Deliveries that arrive with unidentifiable drivers or outside of the expected arrival periods should be scrutinized carefully. If food counterfeiting or tampering seems probable, the CPFM is required to notify the local authorities.

### Vehicle Inspection

The CPFM or the employee receiving a delivery of food products ought to inspect the delivering vehicle. Confirming that the delivery vehicle is sanitary and is kept at an appropriate temperature reduces the risk of illness.

Food deliveries must follow the usual rules and regulations for food storage inside a facility. The delivery container must be kept clean of residue and filth if it presents a serious risk of contaminating the food inside. Food within must be stored appropriately to avoid contamination from dripping, contact with other foods, liquids soaking through packaging, and so on. Although sealed packaging is commonly used in food transportation, the CPFM cannot assume that packaging is infallible.

Trucks that transport temperature-sensitive foods must be insulated and refrigerated so that the container maintains a temperature of 41 °F or below. This keeps the transported food out of the danger zone, especially meat. Often, a truck will maintain a temperature of 0 °F or below to ensure that the food remains fully frozen. A record of the truck's temperature should be kept regularly and be made available to the facility's staff upon request. Confirming that the transported food has remained refrigerated or frozen is an important step in reducing the growth of bacteria that cause foodborne illness.

### Approved Sources

There are many people involved in the food supply chain, from farmers and growers to manufacturing, packing, trucking, and distribution companies. Managers must ensure that their suppliers meet all federal, state, and local laws and regulations. Suppliers must undergo and pass all required safety inspections and should be able to provide evidence of these inspections. Managers can also see the suppliers' inspection reports by contacting the US Food and Drug Administration (FDA) and the US Department of Agriculture (USDA). The inspection report should include information regarding the suppliers' receiving, storage, and processing practices; cleanliness; staff training; and compliance with HACCP, GMP, GAP, or other safety guidelines.

Working with well-known, respected suppliers is the first step to ensuring that the food is free of defects and disease and is safe for human consumption. Developing an ongoing relationship with suppliers and learning about their food safety practices is a solid best practice. One of the most common safety practice guidelines is the Hazard Analysis Critical Control Points (HACCP). HACCP is a food safety management system that is recognized and used worldwide. It assesses food safety through analyzing and controlling physical, biological, and chemical risks. HACCP applies to all stages of food production, starting with raw materials all the way through to handling, manufacturing, and distribution. HACCP guidelines are based upon the foundations established by the Good Manufacturing Practices (GMPs; also referred to as the current Good Manufacturing Practices, or cGMPs).

Food safety practices should be based on the GMPs set forth by the Food and Drug Administration, which are designed to ensure good quality and safety of food products. GMPs are part of the US Code of Federal Regulations (21 CFR 111) and include the five Ps: people, procedures, products, premises, and processes.

The people involved in the process should be well-trained, have clear responsibilities, and be routinely assessed to ensure they are meeting all safety and quality standards. Manufacturing procedures should be standardized, transparent, and routinely reviewed and updated as needed. The products, including both the raw ingredients and the final product, should meet all quality standards and be closely monitored throughout the manufacturing process. The premises, including all equipment used, should be regularly inspected and kept clean and in good working order. Finally, the processes used throughout manufacturing should be continuously reviewed and updated.

The USDA sets forth Good Agricultural Practices (GAP) guidelines for growing produce. GAP guidelines are voluntary, but most reputable farmers and growers opt to adhere to these practices, as they are designed to prevent foodborne illnesses by reducing microbial contamination on farms. The GAP guidelines can be found in the FDA's publication *Guidance for Industry: Guide to Minimize Microbial Food Safety Hazards for Fresh Fruits and Vegetables*.

## Receiving

It is important to inspect deliveries as soon as they arrive. Do not schedule deliveries for times when the manager or staff will be away, busy, or otherwise unavailable to inspect the delivery upon receipt. Employees responsible for delivery receipt and inspection should be properly trained and provided with the necessary equipment to inspect the delivery. This includes any purchase orders or receipts needed to verify that the correct products and amounts are being delivered, scales for weighing produce and other products, and thermometers to ensure items are being kept and delivered at the appropriate temperatures.

Receivers should look at the delivery truck to check for any indications of contamination. Packaging should be inspected to ensure that it is clean, undamaged, and that there are no signs of mistreatment. Use-by dates should also be verified and current. When receiving a delivery that includes time or temperature control for safety (TCS) foods, checking the temperatures of these items is imperative to ensure that they have traveled and arrived at the proper food-safe temperatures. Cold food items such as meats should be 41 °Fahrenheit or cooler. Check fresh meat and poultry by placing a thermometer directly into the thickest part of the meat. Measure vacuum-sealed by placing the thermometer between two packages or, if possible, by folding the package around the thermometer, taking care not to puncture the packaging. Measure other items, such as milk, by inserting the thermometer directly into the product without touching the packaging.

Live and shucked shellfish and milk should arrive at a temperature of 45 °F or cooler; the temperature must be lowered to 41 degrees or cooler within four hours. Shell eggs should have a temperature of 45 degrees or cooler. Frozen foods should be frozen solid upon receipt, and hot foods should have temperatures of at least 137 °F or warmer. Frozen foods that have water or fluid stains on the packaging or have ice crystals on the food should be rejected, as this is evidence of possible thawing and

# Principles of Food Safety

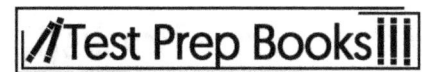

refreezing. When the shipment has been received and approved, the food items, particularly refrigerated and frozen items, should be stored in the appropriate areas immediately.

## Key Drop Deliveries

Sometimes deliveries must be made before or after working hours, when managers and staff may not be on the premises to receive the delivery. In these circumstances, a supplier is given a key or access to the premises to make the delivery. The supplier places the products in freezers, refrigerators, or dry storage areas. This is known as a key drop delivery and should only be permitted from well-respected, trusted suppliers. Key drop deliveries should be inspected immediately when the manager or staff arrives. The receiver should check that the products were delivered to the appropriate storage areas, that they are free of contamination and were protected from contamination when placed in storage, and that they appear to have been delivered with care and according to the purchase order and delivery agreement.

## Accept/Reject Criteria

Sometimes an item or items from a delivery must be rejected. Products that have damaged or torn packaging or packaging that shows evidence of contamination or tampering should be rejected. This includes cans that have bulges, dents, rust, swollen ends, or illegible and/or missing labels, as well as sealed packages that are bloated or leaking. Items with broken seals, damaged cartons, or packaging that is dirty or discolored should also be rejected. Products that show signs of leakage, dampness, water stains, or damage should be rejected, as should any product that shows signs of pests. Additionally, any product that is beyond the use-by or expiration date and any product missing its freshness date should be rejected. Inspect food quality and reject any foods that show signs of mold, pests, discoloration, inappropriate texture (such as sliminess or stickiness), or odors.

Managers and receiving staff must know the proper procedures for handling rejected items. The item should be placed away from the rest of the delivery immediately. Report the issue to the delivery driver and include a detailed description of exactly what is wrong with the item. The delivery driver should provide a signed receipt of adjustment or credit before the item is returned to them. The receiver should also log the incident into the delivery record, either directly on the invoice or purchase order or in the store's delivery records according to the procedure set forth by the manager.

Occasionally, food items may be recalled by the manufacturer. This occurs when there is a problem with the manufacturing process, with the raw ingredients, or with the shipping and handling of the goods. Recalls may also be issued if products are incorrectly labeled, such as omitting allergen warnings that should be present on the packaging. The FDA and USDA issue recall notices, but vendors and suppliers should also notify their customers of any recalls.

Recall items can be identified using the information provided in the recall notice, such as product identification numbers and date, time, and/or location stamps. Once a recall item has been identified, it should be immediately removed from inventory and secured away from the usual food storage areas to prevent accidental use. The item should also be kept away from food prep areas, including utensils and equipment. The item should be clearly marked to avoid accidental use, such as placing a "do not use" sign on the product. The vendor will have specific instructions on how to handle the item, such as disposing of it immediately or returning the item to the vendor.

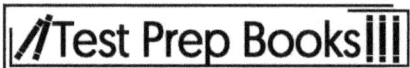

## Critical Control Points (CCPs) and Standard Operation Procedures (SOPs) For the Operation

The CPFM is responsible for analyzing and refining their food service facility's workflow. One important step in this analysis is identifying **critical control points** (CCPs) in the food preparation process. According to the FDA, CCPs are points in the facility's operation where action can be taken that will either prevent, eliminate, or reduce food safety risks to an appropriate level. This concept is found throughout the food preparation process, and many CCPs are already defined by federal or local food regulations. For example, the temperature control requirements for foods such as beef and poultry are each individual CCPs. By heating or cooling those foods appropriately, the facility can take *action* that *prevents* the spread of foodborne illnesses. Another example of a CCP is testing for the presence of environmental or process contaminants before shipping food from a meat packing plant to grocery stores.

Not all CCPs are dictated by government agencies. The CPFM must identify CCPs in the facility's work procedure and determine if action can be taken to further reduce the risk of contamination. For example, this process might require identifying how the facility's physical layout or use of storage creates a situation in which action can be taken to improve outcomes. A specific example might be identifying how food supplies are put into refrigerated storage in such a way that the use of supplies continues to follow the FIFO principle.

All CCPs must be accounted for in the facility's **standard operating procedures** (SOPs). These procedures describe the appropriate workflow in the facility that reduces the risk of food contamination from all sources to as low as possible. While an SOP document may be unable to account for all events that occur in the workplace, the document should comprehensively describe the *typical* procedures required to prepare safe food products.

## Food Safety Systems Training

The **Hazard Analysis Critical Control Point (HACCP) system** provides seven principles that can be used to achieve active managerial control of the five foodborne illness risk factors. The FDA endorses the use of the HACCP principles in general, but an HACCP plan is only mandatory for certain types of facilities. Most retail and food service establishments, however, can choose whether or not to use the HACCP principles as part of their food safety management system.

HACCP principles are meant to be implemented in addition to a strong foundation of **prerequisite programs**—a facility's standard procedures for protecting food from contamination, preventing overgrowth of bacteria, and maintaining equipment on an ongoing basis. These procedures may include specific criteria or processes for vendor certification, employee training, and management of allergens; specific instructions within recipes; and other standard operating procedures (SOPs) such as First In, First Out (FIFO). With prerequisite programs like these in place to promote basic sanitation and safe operations, these seven HACCP principles further promote active managerial control of foodborne illness risk factors.

### Principle 1: Conduct a hazard analysis.
The hazard analysis consists of two parts: hazard identification and hazard evaluation. Food safety hazards may include biological, chemical, or physical hazards.

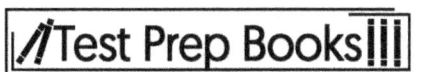

Principles of Food Safety

The particular foods served and preparation processes involved at a given facility will determine what hazards could occur there. These hazards should then be evaluated to determine whether they should be included in the HACCP plan based on their likelihood of occurrence and the severity of the risk they pose. **Control measures** can then be identified to eliminate or reduce the risks of those hazards.

## Principle 2: Determine the critical control points (CCPs).
A **critical control point (CCP)** is a step at which a control measure must be implemented to eliminate a hazard or to reduce it enough to prevent danger.

## Principle 3: Establish critical limits.
Each critical control point has at least one **critical limit**, which is a number that delineates whether or not sufficient reduction or elimination of a hazard has been achieved by the control measure to ensure food safety, such as cooking ground beef to an internal temperature of 155 °F for at least 17 seconds.

## Principle 4: Establish monitoring procedures.
Monitoring procedures are measurements and observations that verify that critical limits are being met and food safety policies are being followed. They may include measuring temperatures or pH levels and observing whether employees are using gloves properly.

## Principle 5: Establish corrective actions.
When a critical limit is not met, a corrective action may involve discarding the food or may provide a way to still ensure the food is safe—for example, by further heating the food until safe limits are met.

## Principle 6: Establish verification procedures.
These are written procedures that lay out the details of how the efficacy of the HACCP plan will be verified, including the specific actions used in verification, who will perform those actions, and how often they will perform them. Verification procedures are distinct from monitoring and may include checking to ensure that monitoring procedures are performed properly, that corrective actions are taken when needed, that monitoring records are accurate and recorded at correct intervals, and that monitoring equipment is functioning properly—such as verifying thermometer calibration.

## Principle 7: Establish record-keeping procedures.
Record-keeping procedures will establish how to document activities that fulfill prerequisite programs and HACCP plan procedures, and these records may prove vital in protecting the food establishment if it is investigated in a foodborne illness case.

## Hazard Communication Requirements

Most food service facilities utilize hazardous materials at some point in routine work duties. These chemicals are typically cleaning supplies. Depending on the type of facility, they may also include industrial lubricants, processing chemicals, or other materials used in food preparation or in maintaining the facility's appliances and equipment.

The Occupational Health and Safety Administration (OSHA) requires communicating all potential hazards to employees working in the facility. This includes hazardous materials that a particular employee may not be expected to work with. For example, a member of the security personnel is unlikely to be involved in food processing or appliance maintenance. As an employee in the facility, they are still potentially exposed to these chemicals in the form of fumes, surface contaminants, and so on.

Consequently, informing employees of the use of these chemicals obtains informed consent about the workplace, improving employee safety and reducing the facility's liability.

As part of this requirement, the facility is also required to keep all chemicals labeled appropriately. The manufacturer's label is generally appropriate. If that label wears off or gets damaged, the CPFM must make sure a new label is applied that describes the chemical and its hazards.

## Hazardous Materials

All chemicals used in a food service facility must be appropriately labeled and stored. Common types of hazardous materials used in a food service facility include:

- Cleaning supplies (sanitizer, dish soap, etc.)
- Maintenance chemicals (oil, hydraulic fluid, etc.)
- Pesticides (bromethalin, strychnine, etc.)
- Processing chemicals (monosodium glutamate, nitrogen gas, etc.)

Additional information about the chemicals must be recorded on the facility's **safety data sheets** (SDS).

The SDS include a variety of terms and symbols to identify a chemical's hazards. These follow an international standard for ease of use. Two signal words are used to describe the chemical: **Warning** indicates a mild hazard, while **Danger** indicates a serious hazard. However, *all* chemicals with a hazard label must be stored and used to the same standards to ensure food safety.

Each SDS also indicates what type of risk is present when using the chemical—health, physical, or environmental risks. Each category has a variety of possible hazards, which are indicated by a hazard icon and described in more detail on the chemical's SDS. The CPFM is able to obtain SDS for all chemicals used in the workplace from that chemical's manufacturer.

## Safe Storage

Hazardous materials should be stored in dry, room-temperature environments (or in another environment if specified by the manufacturer's directions). Best practices require storing chemicals in a locked closet, room, or cabinet so that only employees who need to use the chemicals during routine work duties have access. This reduces the risk of contaminating food by untrained employees accessing the chemicals.

Chemicals and other hazardous materials should be stored at ground level. Placing these materials directly on the floor reduces the risk that they will leak, drip, etc. onto anything placed onto a lower shelf. In particular, hazardous materials must *never* be placed above food supplies or above equipment used in food preparation. This is especially important with cleaning chemicals and processing chemicals used during food preparation, preservation, and packaging. While those chemicals may be stored appropriately in the storage space, employees must use caution to ensure that the chemicals are not also placed above food or food preparation surfaces for temporary storage while the chemical is in use. The CPFM is obligated to train employees to be mindful about where cleaning products and other chemicals are set down in the course of routine work duties. Awareness about temporary storage hazards reduces the risk of contaminating food.

Principles of Food Safety

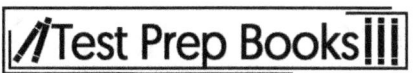

Caution should also be used to ensure that chemicals do not cross-contaminate with one another. Chemicals that interact can result in a variety of hazards, including corrosive liquids, toxic fumes, or explosive fumes. Any time there is a substantial chemical leak discovered in storage, the room should be avoided while the CPFM or the person in charge contacts emergency services for guidance.

**Labels Laws: Facility Use and Disposal of Chemicals**

Waste chemicals produced by a food service facility must be disposed of in compliance with local hazardous material regulations. Most regulations are determined by the Environmental Protection Agency (EPA), but some states have stricter requirements. In particular, the CPFM should consult their local authorities to determine the appropriate disposal of grease.

The Resource Conservation and Recovery Act (RCRA) requires food service facilities to label hazardous materials. This applies to both **listed** waste (types of waste specifically described by RCRA) and **characteristic** waste (the general hazardous properties of the waste product). The disposed waste material must be labeled with the following text: "HAZARDOUS WASTE—Federal Law Prohibits Improper Disposal. If found, contact the nearest police or public safety authority or the U.S. Environmental Protection Agency." Apart from this text requirement, however, the CPFM has liberty to use a label that they feel is appropriate. The label ought to be brightly colored and clearly written to ensure that waste management workers see and understand it.

Proper disposal of hazardous waste generated in food service—especially from industrial facilities—reduces the risk of illness by preventing pollution of the local groundwater. Polluted groundwater or soil has long-term negative effects that impact the facility, the health of its employees, and the health of the local community.

## *Temperature*

**Temperature Danger Zone**

The **danger zone** for any food is the temperature range within which bacteria can grow quickly. For most foods, this range is 41 °F to 135 °F. Even after cooking, bacteria can quickly spread and cause illness in prepared food. The quantity of some bacteria in prepared meals can double in as little as 20 minutes. This is why it's important to ensure that food ready for consumption is delivered promptly to the customer. The USDA recommends that no food should be left unrefrigerated for longer than two hours to mitigate the risk of illness. The CPFM should check their jurisdiction's food safety regulations, because these requirements can vary from state to state. Always follow the strictest safety guideline.

Some common illnesses that can spread from food that is left in the danger zone are *Salmonella*, *E. coli*, and *Campylobacter*. These and other foodborne illnesses share similar symptoms: diarrhea, stomach cramps, fever, and (occasionally) vomiting. Since these bacteria spread more slowly while food is frozen, refrigerated, or remains heated, keeping food out of the danger zone ensures customer safety and reduces the business's risk of litigation.

When considering the danger zone, it's important to be aware of the climate and the working environment. Bacteria spread more quickly in hot temperatures—like, for example, a busy kitchen in the summer! If the temperature in a room used for food preparation or storage exceeds 90 °F, it's important to be especially vigilant about keeping food out of the danger zone. Warm temperatures that aren't over

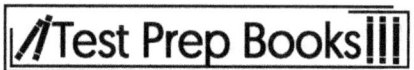

Principles of Food Safety

140 °F encourage the spreading of bacteria. Ensure that food is not left out for longer than an hour when the air temperature exceeds 90 °F.

## Cooking Temperatures

It is important to know the minimum internal temperatures that various foods must be cooked to for safety.

For any kind of raw chicken and turkey, the minimum internal temperature is 165 °F. Pasta, stuffed meat, and stuffing should also reach 165 °F.

Ground pork, beef, lamb, and veal must maintain a minimum internal temperature is 155 °F for 17 seconds to be considered safe. Mechanically tenderized meat like brined ham and shell eggs that will be hot held for service must also reach 155 °F for 17 seconds.

For roasts of pork, beef, lamb, and veal, the minimum internal temperature is 145 °F, which must be maintained for 4 minutes.

All types of fish and shellfish, as well as shell eggs that will be served immediately, must reach a minimum internal temperature of 145 °F for 15 seconds. Steaks and chops of pork, beef, lamb, and veal must also reach 145 °F for 15 seconds.

Plant-based foods like vegetables and grains should be cooked to 135 °F. Tea should be served at 175 °F.

## Heating and Cooling

When preparing and handling food, it's important to make sure the food does not remain in the danger zone for long. This is done most efficiently by heating and cooling food quickly.

Facilities that heat prepared food—such as a soup stock made the previous shift or a prepared meal that was shipped while frozen—must ensure that the heating process is safe. Reheated food must be heated to an internal temperature of at least 165 °F. The CPFM must observe employees to ensure that appropriate reheating processes are followed consistently. These procedures depend on the heating (or reheating) method. For example, when using a microwave oven to reheat an ingredient stored in the refrigerator, it's important to take care that the food is heated evening. Stirring the food or adjusting the plate helps the food reach a consistent internal temperature. Uneven reheating—by any method—risks a portion of the food remaining in the danger zone. Failure to heat food completely gives bacteria an opportunity to spread and cause illness.

After preparing food, it must be cooled below 40 °F for refrigeration. It is permissible to allow food to cool outside the fridge so long as it does not remain in the danger zone for longer than two hours. When cooling prepared food, it is preferable to place it in a wide, shallow bin; tray; or basin. Doing so allows the food to cool evenly, which in turn reduces the time spent in the danger zone before placing it in the fridge or freezer. The refrigerator must be set at 40 °F or lower to maintain food safety. For long-term storage of food, use a freezer set at 0 °F or lower. Merely "below freezing" is not adequate. Food can still spoil while refrigerated, but at 0 °F and below, most bacteria and other causes of spoilage go dormant, allowing for longer storage durations. Do not thaw frozen food at room temperature. Use the fridge instead so that the outside of frozen food does not enter the danger zone while the inside remains frozen.

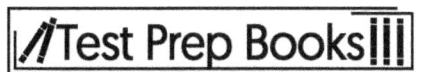

## Holding Temperatures

Facilities that serve ready-to-go hot food—such as buffets—may hold hot food for up to four hours. During this time, the food must be kept at a minimum of 135 °F, although temperatures of 141 °F and higher are preferable to keep the food out of the danger zone. Appropriate devices for maintaining heat include steam tables, holding cabinets, and heated trays. Food should be inspected and stirred frequently. Inspection improves safety by maintaining employee awareness of when the hot food has expired. Stirring does so by helping the food remain consistently at a safe temperature. When hot food is not monitored, the CPFM risks serving unsafe food due to their or their employees' negligence.

Food intended to be served cold—such as a salad—must be stored at a consistent temperature of 40 °F or below. After removing the cold food from the refrigerator, the food is considered safe for up to six hours so long as its temperature does not rise above 70 °F. The CPFM should utilize cold tables, cold crocks, and similar devices to ensure that ready-to-go cold food remains as close to 40 °F as possible. The temperature of cold food should be checked by an employee at least every two hours. Any prepared cold meal or cold tray that has sat out for too long or reached too high a temperature must be discarded.

For both hot and cold food, it's important for the CPFM to implement time management practices in the facility. Maintaining a consistent schedule of when food is set out and when employees must check food reduces the risk of causing foodborne illness. Different practices are best for different facilities. It is the CPFM's job to establish temperature checks as part of the food safety regimen and ensure that they are carried out by the employees.

# Foodborne Illness

## Food Safety Principles

Based on data collected by the US Food and Drug Administration (FDA), in food establishments is dependent on managers taking a proactive approach to controlling foodborne illness risk factors by incorporating specific procedures into the routine operations of the business and monitoring for correct use of those procedures, a concept referred to as **active managerial control**. Some ways to achieve active managerial control include:

- Using purchase specifications listing what items may be purchased and specific quality standards they must meet
- Conducting employee training programs
- Enforcing reporting policies for sick employees
- Implementing standard operating procedures (SOPs) and monitoring procedures
- Using recipes with specific instructions for ensuring that temperature and time requirements are met

## Health Policies and Practices

It is the CPFM's job to evaluate existing health policies, develop new health policies, and ensure that the policies are implemented by their workforce. This reduces the risk of foodborne illness by preventing the spread of disease from employees to the food they handle.

Concerning employees, the CPFM must ensure that all employees report the following symptoms to the employer:

- Vomiting
- Diarrhea
- Jaundice
- Fever
- Open wounds

An open wound is any break in the employee's skin (such as a boil or a cut) through which pus, blood, or another contaminant can leave the body. An employee with such an illness may participate in food preparation if their wound can be completely sealed by a bandage without substantial risk of the covering being torn open.

The other four symptoms listed above are all possible symptoms of a contagious illness. The employer may not permit employees experiencing these symptoms to work in food preparation. If the facility has tasks that do not put the employee in contact with food or with a food service employee, the sick employee is permitted to work in that role.

In addition, the CPFM must make sure that policy requires recording any reported employee illnesses. These records must be made available to local health authorities upon request. If an employee reports a

Foodborne Illness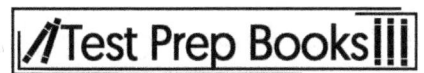

diagnosis of a foodborne illness (such as norovirus or hepatitis A), the policy must require reporting that diagnosis to the local health authority. The CPFM should confirm which diagnoses must be reported based on their local food code.

A food service facility is also required to have policies documenting and reporting instances of customer illness.

## Causes of Foodborne Illnesses

The pathogens that cause foodborne illnesses are a diverse group categorized by type of organism: bacterium, virus, parasite, or fungus.

### Bacteria

Many types of bacteria can cause foodborne illnesses. While most bacteria thrive between 41 °F and 135 °F, some can grow in refrigeration temperatures, some form spores that can survive cooking as part of their life cycle, and some produce toxins that are also heat resistant. The amount of time it takes from ingesting a contaminated food to developing symptoms—the **incubation period**—is most commonly around 12–72 hours, but it can range from 30 minutes to several weeks. Common symptoms include abdominal cramps, nausea, vomiting, fever, and diarrhea that is often watery and, for certain illnesses, bloody. The most important precautions in preventing illnesses caused by bacteria are purchasing food only from approved sources, avoiding cross-contamination of ready-to-eat (RTE) food with juices from raw meat and poultry, cooking food to safe temperatures, washing hands, and excluding sick food employees from work. The following bacteria, commonly spread by farm animals and humans, are especially risky in a food establishment setting.

| Bacteria | Example associated foods |
|---|---|
| *Norovirus* | • Salads<br>• Fresh fruit |
| Shiga toxin-producing *E. coli* (STEC) | • Ground beef<br>• Produce |
| Hepatitis A | • Berries<br>• Shellfish<br>• Salads |
| *Salmonella* Typhi | • RTE foods<br>• Drinks |
| Nontyphoidal *Salmonella* | • Animal products<br>• Produce |
| *Shigella* | • Salads such as potato salad<br>• Produce |

### Viruses

The main viruses responsible for foodborne illnesses are noroviruses and hepatitis A, which are commonly associated with RTE foods and spread primarily via the fecal–oral route; this means virus particles making their way from one person's feces to another person's mouth, either directly from person to person or indirectly through contaminated food or drink. Infected employees, even if asymptomatic, can shed viral particles through their feces that may remain airborne in the restroom for hours, and this is one reason proper hand washing, avoiding bare-hand contact with RTE food, and excluding sick employees from work are such critical steps for preventing foodborne illnesses.

Additionally, bivalve molluscan shellfish—such as clams and oysters—may harbor norovirus and hepatitis A due to contamination from feces in the water they grow in and should only be purchased from approved suppliers. Some viruses, including hepatitis A, can survive cooking temperatures.

Norovirus is the number one cause of foodborne illness in the United States, causing approximately nine hundred deaths per year and leading to the hospitalization of one in 160 children before the age of five. The virus can survive on surfaces for up to two weeks even when subjected to freezing, many chemical disinfectants, and heating to insufficient cooking temperatures. Its symptoms include vomiting, diarrhea, abdominal cramps, nausea, fever, and body aches.

## Parasites

Parasites are organisms that get their nutrition from a host such as a human or other animal. They spread in the form of a cyst and are usually associated with wild game, fish, or products that have been contaminated through water. To prevent parasitic illnesses, food should only be obtained from approved sources and should be cooked or frozen properly, depending on the specific food and use.

Toxoplasmosis, an infection with the parasitic protozoan *Toxoplasma gondii*, is the fourth leading cause of hospitalization and second leading cause of death due to foodborne illness in the United States. It is especially risky for women who are or may become pregnant and for individuals with compromised immune systems. Other notable parasitic illnesses in the US include cryptosporidiosis, cyclosporiasis, giardiasis, and trichinellosis.

## Fungi

Fungi is a classification that includes molds, mushrooms, and yeasts. Molds are microscopic fungi that exist virtually everywhere, grow on plants and animals, and produce spores that travel through the air to plants and animals, where they become established and continue to grow. Most species are harmless, but some molds produce toxins—called **mycotoxins**—that can cause illnesses in humans and animals. Food that is visibly moldy should be thrown out.

A certain amount of mold contamination from the natural environment is considered unavoidable, but government regulatory agencies monitor food products to ensure levels are not too high. One example of a mycotoxin that is monitored by the FDA is aflatoxin, produced by some types of *Aspergillus* molds, which grow on crops such as nuts and grains (like corn and rice). Milk may also contain aflatoxin if the cow ingested it while eating grains. In severe cases, too much aflatoxin can lead to cancer, liver failure, or death.

## Leading Causes of Foodborne illnesses

Data collected by the CDC consistently shows that five **foodborne illness risk factors** are the most significant contributors to foodborne illnesses from retail and food service establishments:

- Food from unsafe sources—such as those from unapproved facilities

- Inadequate cooking (not cooking food to a high enough temperature for a sufficient amount of time to kill or inactivate pathogens)—such as failing to cook fish to an internal temperature of at least 145 °F for at least 15 seconds

- Improper holding times and temperatures—such as holding food in the danger zone for too long

- Contaminated equipment—such as using the same knife or cutting board for raw meat and then for cooked meat without proper cleaning and sanitation in between

- Poor personal hygiene—such as improper or infrequent hand washing

## Reportable Illnesses

To reduce the risk of spreading pathogens, employees must report certain symptoms and diagnoses—referred to as **reportable symptoms** and **reportable diagnoses**—to managers, who then determine whether to **exclude** the employee from the food establishment for a period of time or to **restrict** the employee from working directly with food and food contact equipment such as utensils. When a food employee has jaundice (yellow eyes or skin) or is given a reportable diagnosis—an illness caused by norovirus, hepatitis A, *Shigella*, Shiga toxin-producing *E. coli* (STEC), *Salmonella* Typhi (typhoid fever), or nontyphoidal *Salmonella*—with or without symptoms, the regulatory authority must be notified and must give approval before the employee returns to work.

Additionally, food employees who have potentially been exposed to the following pathogens—through household contact or involvement with a confirmed disease outbreak—within a certain amount of time must be restricted from facilities primarily serving a highly susceptible population (HSP).

- Norovirus—within the past 48 hours
- STEC or Shigella—within the past 3 days
- Salmonella Typhi and Nontyphoidal Salmonella—within the past 14 days
- Hepatitis A—within the past 30 days

| Reportable Symptom | Actions |
|---|---|
| Vomiting or diarrhea | • Exclude until asymptomatic for at least 24 hours OR cleared by medical documentation |
| Jaundice | • Exclude if jaundice first appeared within the past 7 days unless cleared by medical documentation |
| Sore throat with fever | • Exclude from facilities primarily serving an HSP<br>• Restrict in facilities not primarily serving an HSP<br>• Return to work with medical documentation |
| Lesion with pus | • Restrict unless properly covered |

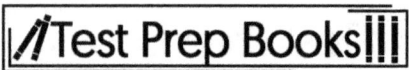

## Potentially Hazardous Foods (PHF), Time/Temperature Control for Safety (TCS)

Most cooked foods and some raw foods can easily become vehicles that harbor and transmit pathogens and toxins to people, resulting in foodborne illness. Managing the temperature and amount of time these foods—referred to as **time/temperature control for safety (TCS) foods**—spend at a given temperature is necessary for limiting pathogen growth and toxin formation. Some examples of TCS foods are:

- Cooked or raw beef, pork, fish, and chicken
- Cooked fruits and vegetables
- Cooked grains, such as pasta and rice
- Raw, cut melons, tomatoes, and leafy greens
- Ready-to-eat foods such as potato salad, pizza, and casseroles

In most cases, it is important to cook TCS food to the temperature recommended for that food and to limit the amount of time it spends in the **danger zone** between 41 °F (5 °C) and 135 °F (57 °C). Much like humans, pathogens do best when they are not too hot and not too cold, so they will thrive and multiply within the danger zone. The less time TCS foods are allowed to remain within this temperature range, the less likely they will be able to make someone sick. When cooling food below 135 °F, the temperature must drop from 135 °F to 70 °F (21 °C) within two hours and from 135 °F to 41 °F within six hours. If food is prepared with room-temperature ingredients, such as shelf-stable canned goods, the prepared food must be cooled to 41 °F within four hours. Food with a greater mass or volume and food that is covered will take longer to cool, but cooling times can be reduced using a variety of methods, such as stirring the food in a container placed in an ice water bath, using rapid cooling equipment, or maximizing the exposed surface area by using larger or multiple containers. In circumstances where TCS foods are delivered to the food establishment, monitoring to ensure proper temperature control both upon arrival and during the transportation process also help ensure food safety. Ready-to-eat TCS foods that will not be sold or consumed within 24 hours must be clearly marked with the date by which they should be consumed or sold. When refrigerated, this is 7 days after being prepared.

## Cooking, Holding, Cooling, and Reheating Procedures

One area of concern with holding food is cooling. The best way to properly cool foods is through two steps. Foods should reach 70 °F within two hours and, following this, should reach 41 °F within four hours (total time from the beginning of the cooling process).

## Food Protection

It is important to inspect your produce before preparation and consumption. Any produce that appears rotten should be thrown out, and damaged parts of the produce should be removed. When preparing produce, it should be thoroughly rinsed. Produce does not need to be washed with soap in order to be cleaned. Even if the skin of the fruit is not going to be eaten, it should still be rinsed. If the fruit has a rind, such as cantaloupe, it should be scrubbed. This is done to prevent bacteria from transferring to the inside of the fruit upon being cut or peeled. After being rinsed, produce should be dried to further lessen the bacteria on its surface. This can be done with a paper towel or a clean towel.

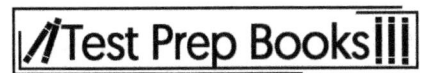

## Self-Service Protection

Self-service food environments (such as buffets) increase the risk of foodborne illness due to the exposure of food to the public. Appropriate equipment, self-service tools, and signage can reduce the risk of foodborne illness.

Self-service equipment should be heated or chilled—as appropriate to the served food—to keep it out of the danger zone. Food should be separated from direct contact with customers by a sneeze guard, cabinet door, or other suitable method. This reduces the risk of airborne pathogens contaminating the food.

Customers should always be required to use the provided self-service tools. Signs reminding customers to use tongs, spoons, paper napkins, or other instruments increase the frequency with which said tools are used. Avoiding contact with hands reduces the chance of disease. Reusable tools should be sanitized or replaced regularly. Likewise, any plates and utensils taken by customers should not be reused when accessing self-service stations multiple times. Repeated use risks contamination by returning germs to the food area. When possible, single-use tools (such as paper napkins) are preferred because they reduce the risk of contamination through repeated use. Covering ready-to-eat food in paper or foil wrapping also improves food safety by limiting the food's exposure after it leaves the kitchen.

## Foodborne Illness Symptoms

Foodborne illnesses are mainly caused by either a foodborne infection or a foodborne intoxication. **Foodborne infections** are illnesses in which pathogens themselves—like *E. coli* bacteria or the hepatitis A virus—make a person sick.

**Foodborne intoxications** are illnesses caused by toxins, including:

- Naturally occurring toxins that accumulate in seafood from the water and from other animals it ingests

- Toxins produced by pathogens, including *Bacillus cereus*, *Clostridium botulinum*, *Staphylococcus aureus*, and *Aspergillus*

- Chemicals added to foods unintentionally through the use of chemicals at any point in the production process, including pesticides, fertilizers, and cleaning products

- Substances added to food as preservatives

- Heavy metals from the environment—like mercury—or those like copper and lead that leach into food from utensils or from the vessels in which it is stored

The symptoms of foodborne intoxications often involve vomiting and diarrhea and typically develop more quickly than symptoms of foodborne infections.

In addition to foodborne infections and foodborne intoxications, consumers may also be in danger if physical contaminants—including bone fragments and foreign objects—are introduced into the food within the food establishment or in some previous supply chain step (e.g., in its source environment, during processing, during packaging). This creates risks like broken teeth, choking, cuts, bleeding, infection, and the need for surgical removal.

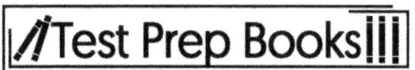

## Chemical Contaminants

Two types of chemicals most frequently are found in food: **environmental contaminants** and **process contaminants.**

Environmental contaminants enter food through the environment in which the food was grown. Common examples include arsenic, mercury, and lead. The source of most environmental contaminants is soil or water that contained the contaminant—whether from a natural or an industrial source—and then entered the ecosystem.

Process contaminants are chemicals that are formed in foods after processing. The most common processes that can create these contaminants are heating, drying, and fermenting. Some of the more common contaminants include **furan**, which forms when heating food during canning; **acrylamide**, which forms in potatoes and grain-based foods when frying; and **ethyl carbamide**, which forms during beverage fermentation.

Chemical contaminants can affect those who consume them in a wide variety of ways, and research on human tolerance and safe consumption is often ongoing. The CPFM is expected to educate themselves about potential contaminants that may be found in their food service facility. A fast-food restaurant and a beverage bottling plant have different chemical contaminant risks! However, the risk from both types of contaminants is minimal so long as the CPFM ensures that the facility is aware of the source of its supplies and routinely tests its food for chemical presence.

The **Food and Drug Administration** (FDA) regulates what presence of these contaminants is acceptable and safe in food. These regulations typically allow a particular rate in **parts per million** (ppm) or **parts per billion** (ppb). A rate of 10 ppm means that out of one million molecules, only ten may be from the contaminant. These strict requirements are important because in addition to typical foodborne illness symptoms, the presence of chemical contaminants can have serious effects such as cancer or arrested development in children.

## Chemicals Storage

The CPFM must take precautions that any chemicals stored on-site are not stored or used near food. This includes both food preparation and food storage. Any room used to store food may not also be used to store hazardous chemicals, even if the chemicals are kept in a separate cabinet or adjoining closet. While such circumstances may in general avoid contamination, they increase the risk of an accident in chemical usage, which can result in contaminating the stored food.

Proper storage requires keeping all chemicals in a separate storage room, closet, etc. This space should be locked, so that only employees who have received appropriate training can access the chemicals. All chemicals must be labeled clearly. If a label wears off or becomes faded, it is the CPFM's responsibility to make sure a new label is made for the sake of safety. The storage space must be labeled as well to ensure that all employees are aware what is in the room.

Further, all chemicals must be stored in accordance with the manufacturer's directions. In most cases, these directions specify a temperature maximum or minimum within which the chemical can be safely stored (sort of like the chemical's "danger zone" when compared with food). One common cause of risk when storing chemicals is placing them near furnaces, boilers, or other warm and hot appliances in a janitorial space. If the air temperature is within the manufacturer's specifications, it is permissible to store the chemical in a furnace room so long as distance is maintained between the chemicals and any heat sources.

If a chemical is removed from storage for use, it should never be set down on or above a food preparation surface. When cleaning a surface with chemicals, the CPFM or their employees should make sure that any lower surfaces, drawers, etc. are also cleaned to avoid contamination. This reduces the risk of foodborne illness through dried chemicals coming into contact with raw food.

Risks when chemicals are not stored appropriately include contaminating food and creating noxious fumes. These present a serious risk to the health of customers and employees alike.

## Corrective Action for Contamination Occurrences

Procedures and employee training must be in place in case of a foodborne illness outbreak. If an outbreak is suspected, the following actions will help prevent additional cases and aid authorities in determining the cause.

- Collect important data from the ill person, including symptoms, food eaten, and contact information.

- Close the facility to avoid additional exposure to whatever food may be causing infection.

- Contact the local regulatory entity, such as the city health department. Explain the issue, respond to follow-up questions fully and honestly, and encourage employees' full cooperation.

- Collect information from food employees and document who was working when the suspected outbreak occurred.

- Label, set aside, and document details about any food implicated in the illness, and avoid throwing away other food in case it is needed.

## Documentation

Any instance of foodborne illness must be rigorously documented. This is not merely a regulatory requirement—it helps the CPFM do their job! Prompt documentation of illness provides the CPFM with data by which they can attempt to track potential sources of illness and enact changes to reduce risk. This improves safety and quality, and reduces their facility's liabilities.

Before developing a documentation procedure, the CPFM ought to consult their local jurisdiction's requirements. Some states require use of a provided form, while others simply require reporting illness to a government hotline. The symptoms and illnesses that must be reported may also vary from place to place. The facility's documentation procedure must be in compliance with the *strictest* applicable regulation.

Appropriate documentation of an illness requires the following:

- Date of documentation
- Name of the person writing
- Name of the symptomatic person
- Symptoms experienced

- Date the symptoms began
- Diagnosis of a medical professional, if any

Including this information helps track similar illnesses through similar symptoms and incubation periods. It also helps track contacts between persons, which can help indicate whether or not the illness is foodborne.

## Major Foods That Cause Most Allergic Reactions

There are nine **major food allergens:** milk, eggs, fish, crustacean shellfish, tree nuts, wheat, peanuts, soybeans, and sesame. The majority of food allergy reactions are caused by an immune system response to proteins in these foods or foods derived from them.

## Allergic Reactions and Symptoms

Symptoms from allergic reactions usually appear within anywhere from a few minutes to two hours and may include:

- Itching, rashes, or hives
- Dwelling of some part of the body, such as the lips, tongue, or face
- Breathing difficulty, cough, or throat tightness
- Feeling dizzy or lightheaded
- Gastrointestinal distress, such as vomiting, nausea, abdominal pain, or diarrhea
- Anaphylactic shock, which can result in death

Even a very small amount of an allergen can be problematic or dangerous, and cross-contact of allergen-containing foods with other foods is a common cause of reported food allergy reactions. Studies indicate that while employees may be very happy to accommodate allergy-related requests, many do not have adequate training about food allergies, and some believe that a very small amount of the allergen will not cause a reaction. Having a system in place to clearly and accurately inform customers of the presence of potential food allergens—by providing them with ingredient lists or recipes, for example—and to prevent cross-contact—by preparing their meals in a freshly, thoroughly cleaned or separate, allergen-free area, for example—will enable them to safely enjoy their meal.

## Customer Notifications

To avoid causing preventable illnesses, all food service facilities must notify customers of potential hazards. These notices must be placed on the food's packaging, menu, or a similar easily visible and readable source. In some jurisdictions, food information must be provided in additional languages upon request.

The facility is required to disclose any allergens to which its food may be exposed during the food preparation process. Even if an allergen is not an ingredient in the food, it's important to list allergens handled by the facility. This appropriately informs the customer of the risk and also reduces the facility's liability for an allergen-related illness. All potential food allergens in a product (such as peanuts, shellfish, etc.) must be listed on the label.

It's also important to notify customers about the risks of consuming partially cooked or undercooked foods. This is especially true for facilities that serve beef, pork, chicken and eggs, or fish. Providing this

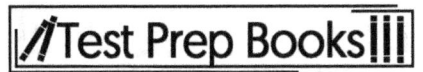

Foodborne Illness

notice informs the customer of standard risks of purchasing and consuming those foods. It reminds the customer to report uncooked food to the facility and reduces the facility's liability for illness.

Food service facilities are also required to disclose nutrition information about their products. The exact requirements vary, depending on the type of facility. In the United States, most facilities must now report the caloric value of their meals, and at minimum provide a list of ingredients and other nutrition information (such as the amount of fat or carbohydrates in the food) upon request.

## Food Labels

One of the most important aspects of food storage is proper labeling. Food must be labeled to prevent confusion (such as mistaking one food item for another) and allergen contamination. Items in their original containers are likely already sufficiently labeled, but items that are removed from their original containers must be properly labeled. Labels should include the common name of the item, such as "flour," as opposed to a brand name that might not be immediately recognized. Labels could also include a photo of the item for easy identification. While it may not always be necessary to label foods that could not be mistaken for anything else, labeling everything is a good habit for safety.

## Methods to Clean and Sanitize Food Contact Surfaces (FCS)

Many measures must be taken to maintain the cleanliness and safety of self-service bars. Any self-serve areas should be monitored closely to ensure cleanliness. When food is brought out to the self-serve area from the kitchen, it should be covered as it is brought out. When replacing food, new food should not be mixed with old food; rather, the whole container should be replaced. Certain things should not be placed within the container, such as food that has been previously handled, objects, and the handles of serving utensils. When it comes to serving utensils, only clean utensils should be used in serving food. Anything that is contaminated, whether it be utensils or food, should be removed immediately. Food should be protected from coughs and sneezes to help prevent it from becoming contaminated. One way to protect food from this is to have a barrier such as a sneeze guard. Customers should be encouraged to use sanitary practices through means such as signs posted around the self-serve area to make these practices clear. Other sanitary practices for customers to participate in involve dishware and utensils. Plates should not be used more than once. Utensils that will be used for eating should be grabbed by the handle, and they should be stored in a way that customers first grab them by the handle. Finally, temperatures of foods should be monitored to ensure they are staying within safe zones for consumption. Cold foods should be held below 41 °F. Hot foods should be held at 135 °F and above.

Open containers and condiments should be monitored for their cleanliness. When empty, open bottles of condiments should be replaced, not refilled. Some condiments, due to contamination risks when they are served in open containers, must be thrown away at the end of the business day. Certain condiments must be refrigerated during non-business hours. The shelf lives of opened and unopened condiments must be monitored as well. Mayonnaise can last for around three months unopened at room temperature and, once opened, must be refrigerated and used within two months. Mayonnaise cannot be left opened and unrefrigerated for more than two hours; this runs the risk of contamination. Certain condiments are safe to keep unrefrigerated once opened, but they do not last nearly as long as refrigerated condiments. For example, ketchup can be unopened at room temperature for around one year. Once opened, it can last for around six months refrigerated. However, if ketchup is opened and unrefrigerated, it can last for around one month.

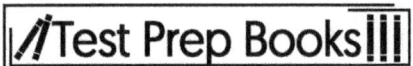

## Labeling Techniques for Date Marking and Identifying Foods in Storage

In addition to labeling for identification, labels should also include freshness date information. Even refrigerated foods can contain bacteria, such as *Listeria monocytogenes*, that is harmful and can cause illness. Ready-to-eat TCS foods must be labeled carefully, particularly if they will be stored for longer than twenty-four hours. Ready-to-eat TCS foods cannot be stored for longer than seven days and must maintain a temperature of 41 °F or cooler. The seven-day time frame begins on the day the food was prepared for consumption or the date the sealed container was first opened. The "prepared," "use by," or "discard" date should be clearly indicated on the label. Foods that contain ingredients with varying use-by dates should be marked according to the earliest date. For example, if a container of potato salad is prepared on March 20, but the mayonnaise used in the salad has a use-by date of March 25, then the use-by date on the label should be March 25, even though that is earlier than seven days from the date of preparation. It is always better to err on the side of caution regarding freshness dates.

## Internal Audit

The CPFM should inspect and audit their facility on a regular basis. Using a combination of scheduled and unscheduled inspections encourages consistent health and safety standards through improving employee vigilance.

During an audit, the CPFM ought to physically inspect the facility and examine the facility's documentation.

While physically inspecting the facility, the CPFM is looking for potential causes of foodborne illness. This ranges from making sure employees are consistently following handwashing and sanitation practices to inspecting the cleanliness of food preparation equipment and food storage locations. Avoid performing a cursory inspection by making sure to open drawers, inspect the interior of any appliances and machinery, examine the cleanliness of shelving, and so on. A rigorous inspection ensures that proper sanitation standards are being met. Doing so reduces the risk of illness through the proliferation of bacteria and other pathogens.

To audit the facility's documentation, the CPFM must compare all reported causes of injury to other sources of information. For example, if an employee reported illness, confirm that employee used a sick day. If the report lists one date but the sick day is listed for another, there is an error in the data. Auditing the documentation for completion is effective, but comparing multiple sources of information helps the CPFM reduce errors and improve accuracy.

# Food Safety Education

## Employee Training

Because each of the five major foodborne illness risk factors is a result of human error, food workers are the frontline defenders in protecting their customers from foodborne illness. While it would be great if people did everything they were taught to do, this is often not the case. Most people have heard of the importance of regular exercise, plenty of sleep, and eating their vegetables, yet ever-increasing rates of lifestyle-related diseases confirm what most know from experience: knowing doesn't always translate to doing.

Knowledge of food safety is only beneficial if the employee actually uses it. Research shows that giving employees information through knowledge-based training is not as effective in changing their behaviors as behavior-based training, which incorporates elements that motivate learners by addressing their attitudes and beliefs. In fact, during peak times, knowledge-based training alone can have no significant impact, while behavior-based training does.

Here are some strategies to improve the efficacy of food safety training.

- Tailor training to the audience by considering trainees' learning preferences, styles, and aptitudes. For example, incorporating a combination of auditory, visual, and tactile elements into the training helps engage students with different learning styles or with limited English proficiency.

- Explain why it is important to practice food safety activities and report illnesses, and consider sharing current, local foodborne illness cases.

- Avoid overly long training sessions.

- Schedule refresher training at least once per year.

- Incorporate ongoing observation and feedback to acknowledge compliant behaviors and correct noncompliance.

- Foster motivation and employees taking pride in their work through methods such as rewards and goal setting.

- Provide mentoring to increase employees' confidence in their ability to put food safety measures into practice.

- Set a good example.

It is common for food handlers to believe that they must choose to either practice food safety or actually get their jobs done. This may help explain why food safety behaviors tend to decrease during peak times. Fostering a culture that emphasizes, reinforces, rewards, and models food safety practices is essential to preventing foodborne illness.

## Unsafe Food Handling Practices

There are various types of glassware and dishes, and it is important to know how to properly handle them. Generally, glassware and dishes should be handled gently. One important thing to remember about glass is to be careful about temperature. Glass cannot move too quickly between very hot and very cold temperatures since this can lead to glass breaking (thermal shock). Glass must be allowed to reach room temperature before being brought to very hot or very cold temperatures. Glass can also be made more susceptible to damage through coming into contact with other objects. It is generally impossible to tell the integrity of glass by visual means; it is important to attempt to limit glass coming into contact with other objects to maintain its integrity. Glassware should not be carried in multiples at a time to avoid damage through contact. Stacking glasses should also be avoided since this could result in many glasses being broken if the pile of glasses is knocked over; in addition, stacking glasses causes the glasses to come into contact with one another. There are also things to keep in mind regarding washing glassware. Glassware should be allowed to cool after coming out of the dishwasher to help prevent thermal shock from occurring. Another important thing to keep in mind for washing glassware in a dishwasher is to ensure that glassware is placed on the correct rack and to keep glassware from touching each other. Cold glasses should be allowed to warm up to room temperature by dumping out any ice remaining in them before going through a dishwasher or washing by hand. When washing dishes by hand, avoid letting glassware rest in the water. This prevents the glass from hitting the bottom of the sink or other dishes and glassware within the sink. Glasses should not be used if they are cracked or have a chip in them. Glasses should also be stored properly. Dishes, glasses, and utensils must be handled with care, particularly when they are being served. Plates should be held in the palm, and fingers should be placed under the plate or along the edge of the plate, avoiding contact with food. Utensils should be held only by the handle. Glasses should never be carried by their rim.

## Cross-Contamination Prevention Practices

In storing food from a shipment, cross-contamination should be avoided. Ensure that foods are kept separate and held properly. One practice that helps with the storing of food is keeping older food more accessible to ensure they are used before going bad. Also, raw foods should not be stored on top of foods that are ready-to-eat to avoid raw foods dripping down onto the ready-to-eat foods. Foods should be held outside of the temperature danger zone. Make sure that hot-held and cold-held foods stay within the appropriate safe temperature ranges. To do so, the temperatures of these foods should be monitored.

## Methods to Clean and Sanitize

While the terms *cleaning* and *sanitizing* are sometimes used interchangeably, it is important to understand the difference between them. Cleaning removes surface dirt, debris, food particles, and other undesirable material from surfaces. Sanitizing involves the use of chemicals to remove bacteria from surfaces. Disinfecting goes a step further and removes bacteria and viruses from surfaces. Specific products are needed for sanitization and disinfecting surfaces, while usually a combination of water and soap or detergent is sufficient for cleaning. Cleaning is usually enough for non-food-contact surfaces, such as walls, floors, and storage shelves. Sanitization is required for any surface, utensil, or equipment used in food preparation. All food contact surfaces should be cleaned and sanitized when changing to prepare a different kind of food, whenever a task is interrupted and the surface may have become contaminated, after use, and every four hours during continuous use.

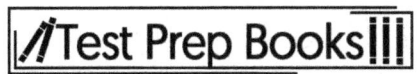

# Cleaning

To clean surfaces, any stuck-on materials need to be removed using a brush, pad, or clean cloth. Then the surface should be washed using an appropriately mixed cleaning soap or detergent. The surface should be scrubbed with some vigor, making sure that the soap fully covers the surface. Next, rinse the surface with clean water. Depending on the surface, this can be done by pouring clean water over the surface or by wiping the surface with a clean, wet cloth. Once the surface is rinsed, it is usually a good idea to dry the surface with another clean cloth.

There are four major types of cleaners: detergents, delimers, degreasers, and abrasive cleaners. Each type of cleaner serves a different purpose but may share some ingredients with other cleaners. Detergents can be used for most cleaning tasks; they work to remove dirt and grime from surfaces. Delimers are specifically made to remove mineral deposits and other types of residue, often left by hard water and buildup. Degreasers have components that help to dissolve grease and are usually used in areas that get very greasy. Abrasive cleaners are usually used to scrub off food or stuck-on objects from other equipment.

There are two types of wiping cloths: wet and dry. Wet cloths are used with sanitizing solution to wipe down surfaces and equipment. Dry cloths are used for food spills. It's important that the two cloths are only used for their specific purposes.

# Sanitizing

Heat sanitization and chemical sanitization are the two primary methods of sanitizing surfaces. Heat sanitization involves heating the surface to at least 171 °F and soaking the surface for at least thirty seconds. This type of sanitization works best for items that can be submerged, such as utensils. Chemical sanitizers can be applied by soaking the surfaces or by spraying, swabbing, or otherwise applying the chemical to the surface. The most common sanitizing chemicals are chlorine, iodine, and quaternary ammonium compounds. Chemical sanitizers are closely regulated by the EPA and should always be used carefully according to the manufacturer's directions.

Sanitizers must be used correctly to be effective. Key aspects of correct use include the concentration of the sanitizer, temperature, pH, water hardness, and the length of time the sanitizer is in contact with the surface.

## Concentration

Concentration involves the appropriate mix of sanitizer and water. Concentration is measured in parts per million (ppm) and should be checked against the test kit that is usually included with the product. Having the correct concentration is critical to the effectiveness of the sanitizer. Too much water results in a weak mixture that may not effectively sanitize the surface, and too little water results in a strong mixture than could be hazardous. Always mix sanitizer in accordance with the manufacturer's instructions.

## Temperature

Sanitizing concentrate should be mixed with water that is a suitable temperature to ensure that the chemicals are sufficiently diluted. Using water that is too cold can result in a separated solution, while using water that is too hot could cause the chemicals to break down and become less effective. Water temperatures should be between 68 and 100 °F, depending on the chemical being used. If using iodine,

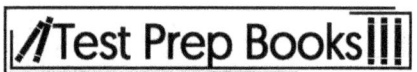

the proper water temperature is 68 °F, for quats, the water temperature should be 75 °F. Mixing chlorine, the water temperature should be at least 75 °F for water that has a pH of 8 or less, and at least 100 °F for water that has a pH of 10 or less.

### Water Hardness and pH
Water hardness refers to the level of minerals in the local water, and pH refers to the level of acidity in the water. This information can be obtained from the local water company, and the sanitizer manufacturer can provide information as to the suitable concentrate for these conditions.

### Time
The final key to effective sanitization is making sure that the sanitizer is in contact with the surface for enough time. The amount of time necessary to fully sanitize a surface depends on the chemical being used and ranges from seven to thirty seconds. For chlorine, it's at least seven seconds, and for both iodine and quats it's at least thirty seconds.

To sanitize a surface, the surface must first be cleaned using the techniques described above. Once the surface is clean, a properly mixed sanitizer should be applied. The manufacturer's label should include directions for mixing the concentration into a usable solution as well as instructions for applying the sanitizer. It is important to make sure that the sanitizer thoroughly covers the entire surface. Once the surface has been fully sanitized, allow it to air dry.

### Preparation for Cleaning
The correct way to clean and sanitize equipment depends on the type of equipment. Thoroughly review the manufacturer's instructions and recommendations prior to cleaning the equipment to ensure that nothing is damaged by incompatible cleaning products and that no one is injured through misuse of the equipment.

Any motorized or electrical equipment must be unplugged for safety prior to cleaning. Remove any parts of the equipment that can be removed for cleaning, such as the blades on a slicer. Wash, rinse, and sanitize those by hand or by running them through a dishwasher, if permitted.

For immovable parts of the equipment, scrape any food scraps away. Wash the equipment using a brush, towel, or other appropriate cleaning tool. Rinse the surface using another clean cloth or towel. Apply the sanitizing solution according to the manufacturer's instructions and ensure that the solution comes into contact with all the equipment's surfaces. Allow to air dry before reassembling the machine.

Machines that hold and dispense ready-to-eat TCS foods, such as ice cream machines and soda machines, should be cleaned daily according to the manufacturer's directions and local regulations. This usually involves running a cleaning and/or sanitizing solution through the machine.

# Facilities and Equipment

## Methods to Clean and Sanitize

Staff should be trained to properly clean and sanitize surfaces, equipment, and utensils. The first step to clean and sanitize surfaces is removing or scraping off any food that is on the surface. Before sanitizing the surface, it should be cleaned. This should be done with a cleaning solution and can aid in removing leftover residue. After a cleaning solution is used, the surface should be rinsed in order to remove the solution and ensure the surface can be properly sanitized. The next step is to sanitize the surface. Different restaurants use different sanitizing solutions (such as sanitizers that are quaternary-based). The sanitizer should be spread with a disposable wipe, not a paper towel or reusable cloth; they can both absorb the sanitizer and limit how well it can be spread across the surface. The sanitizer should be spread over the surface and allowed to air dry for at least one minute.

To clean and sanitize equipment, first shut off and unplug the equipment. Any removable parts can be removed and then washed, either with the dishwasher or by hand. Just like when cleaning and sanitizing surfaces, equipment surfaces must be wiped of debris before being washed with a cleanser. This cleanser should be rinsed off for the sanitizer to be applied to the equipment. The equipment and its removable parts should then be allowed to air dry before putting them back together.

## Schedule(s) for Cleaning and Sanitizing

The frequency with which appliances and equipment should be cleaned in a food service facility depends on the object's use. Once the CPFM has determined a suitable cleaning regimen, they should post it in the facility as a reminder to employees. A checklist, schedule, or other document improves sanitation consistency by describing the standards required.

Equipment that comes into direct contact with raw food that requires temperature controls (such as raw meat) must be cleaned before each use, including when changing between different types of raw food, like chopping beef and then chopping chicken. This rule applies to all types of equipment, ranging from common kitchen knives to meat slicers or other appliances utilized in industrial facilities. However, if the food preparation area is refrigerated, the cleaning regimen may be less frequent. This exception is permitted due to the effect of refrigeration on slowing the growth and spread of bacteria. The required frequency depends on the facility's documented air temperature:

- 41 °F or less: Every 24 hours
- 41 °F to 45 °F: Every 20 hours
- 45 °F to 50 °F: Every 16 hours
- 50 °F to 55 °F: Every 10 hours

If the air temperature is above 55 °F, the equipment must be cleaned before it is used again in food preparation.

Equipment that is used either to serve ready-to-eat food or to handle non-temperature-sensitive foods (such as flour for baking) must be cleaned at least once every 24 hours. This rule also applies to microwave ovens. A microwave oven must be fully cleaned every 24 hours, including the door seals and any cavities in the interior. Other equipment that must be cleaned on this schedule includes tongs or ladles used in self-service, steam tables, etc.

Any equipment used in food service but *not* used in food preparation must be cleaned frequently enough to avoid buildup of residue or filth. This includes refrigerators, storage racks, and so on.

## Ware Washing Equipment and Temperatures

Dishes, flatware, and glass can be run through the dishwasher. Both a chemical and high-temperature dishwasher sanitize dishes, although through different methods. For items that contact food but are unable to be washed in the dishwasher (such as pans), a three-compartment sink can be used. The first compartment is used for cleaning, the second for rinsing, and the third for sanitizing. First, any food that is left on the dishes should be scraped off. Then, the dishes can be cleaned by scrubbing them in warm and soapy water. After this, they can be rinsed in the second compartment with warm water before being placed in the sanitizing compartment. The water in the first and second compartments must be a minimum of 110 °F. After they are sanitized, they should be air dried.

Dishwashers clean and sanitize tools and equipment using both heat and chemicals. High-heat dishwashers heat the water to between 165 °F and 180 °F, depending on the type of machine. The dishwasher should have a built-in thermometer that shows the high temperature, and care should be taken to ensure that the machine is in correct working order. Otherwise, it may not effectively sanitize the dishes. Usually, plates, utensils, and small equipment parts can be cleaned in a dishwasher, while large pots and pans and other types of equipment must be cleaned and sanitized by hand.

As with other types of equipment, dishwashers must also be kept clean and well maintained. The machine should be checked daily to ensure that it is free of food and debris, that all spray nozzles are clean and in good working order, and that there are no mineral deposits.

Dishes must be properly prepped and loaded into the dishwasher for optimal cleaning. Scrape away any remaining food debris, ensuring that there are no stuck-on foods. Load the dishes so that the spray will reach all the dish surfaces, and never overload the machine. When the wash and rinse cycles have finished, allow the dishes and utensils to air dry. Drying with a towel or other cloth could cause recontamination.

## Manual Washing

Tools and equipment, such as large pots and pans and serving platters, may require handwashing. This should be done using a three-basin sink. Each basin should be thoroughly cleaned prior to washing dishes. The first basin should be filled with an appropriate mixture of soap and water at least 110 °F. The second basin should be filled with clean water or left open if a sprayer will be used to rinse the dishes. The third sink basin should be filled with the appropriate sanitizing mixture or suitably hot water for sanitizing. It is also helpful to have a clock with a second hand nearby so sanitization times can be monitored. Once dishes are washed, rinsed, and sanitized, they should be allowed to air dry to avoid recontamination.

Three-basin sinks should also be of suitable size and should be well-maintained. Sinks should be large enough to clean large pots and pans, dishes, and other equipment and should be kept clean and sanitized regularly. Check for and repair any water leaks immediately.

## Hood Vents and Filter Cleaning Requirements

Smoke, grease, and other byproducts of food preparation can become airborne during food preparation processes. These byproducts are cycled out of the kitchen by hood vents over cooking appliances and, in some facilities, additional vents in the ceiling. Cycling out contaminated air and pulling in clean air improves food safety and workplace safety by reducing the risk of illness or fire due to pollutants. However, these pollutants can stick to the filter, fans, or ductwork of the vent system and can commonly cause serious kitchen fires if ignited. Buildup also reduces the efficacy of the system, resulting in poor air quality in work spaces. This can cause employee illnesses for which the facility is liable.

As with other food preparation appliances, hood vents must be made of a smooth and nonporous material for the ease of cleaning—typically stainless steel. The system must be built in accordance with the National Fire Protection Association's (NFPA) Standard 96. This rule specifies the standard to which the manufacturer must build a hood vent for use in food service operations.

To clean a hood vent, first turn off the vent and *all* nearby appliances—even if the vent isn't directly above them. Allow the kitchen to completely cool, and then begin to disassemble the vent. Remove the filters and the grease traps and allow them to soak in a combination of water and degreaser. The amount of time depends on the pollutant buildup, but at least three hours is typical. Once the filter and grease traps are removed, the fan is accessible for removal and cleaning. Before reassembling the hood vent, clean the duct above the vent as far as is safely possible. Fully cleaning a duct system typically requires hiring a professional contractor.

The NFPA advises cleaning a hood vent system at least quarterly for most food service facilities. Depending on the fuel used and the frequency with which the vent is used, cleaning can be scheduled more or less frequently.

## Safe Food Flow

The concept of **food flow** describes how food enters a facility from the supplier, is prepared, and is then delivered to the customer. Designing the physical environment—typically a kitchen—with food flow in mind improves safety by reducing the risk of contamination in fully prepared food.

The basic food flow process requires designing the food preparation area in a linear manner:

- Supply delivery
- Food storage
- Food preparation
- Food delivery

This food flow reduces risk by keeping raw food near the back of the facility, and improves efficiency by keeping prepared food close to the point of delivery. Complement safe food flow in the kitchen with an appropriate flow of dirtied utensils, plates, and food service equipment. Returning used equipment to a designated location establishes a second linear flow in which the equipment is cleaned and then returned to the food preparation area.

When designing a kitchen's layout, organize appliances so that the food flow and the dishes flow do not cross. This reduces the risk of workplace accidents resulting in injury or food contamination (such as an employee holding prepared food bumping into an employee carrying dirty dishes).

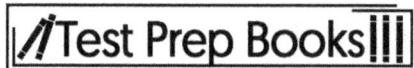

Facilities and Equipment

## Safe Practices

Handwashing stations should be readily accessible, including stations in and/or directly adjacent to restrooms. Stations should also be available in food prep areas, food service areas, and near dishwashing areas. All handwashing stations should be clean and well-stocked. This means always having potable hot and cold water, soap, and either paper towels, a continuous towel system, or an air dryer for drying hands. Handwashing stations should not be used for any other purpose, such as storing dirty dishes or other equipment. These stations should not be blocked by equipment or other items.

## Requirements for Separate Rooms and/or Safe Storage

A food service facility has multiple requirements for storage, depending on what is being stored. The specific regulations vary from one location to another. It is the CPFM's duty to make sure their facility remains compliant with the strictest applicable standard.

Separate storage spaces are required for the following supplies:

- Raw food
- Unopened deliveries
- Hazardous chemicals
- Garbage and waste

Equipment used in food preparation is not required to be stored in a separate and distinct location. However, it may not be stored where there is risk of contamination (such as in a delivery room, under a stairwell, in a janitorial closet, etc.). In most circumstances, it is appropriate to store food preparation equipment in the same area as food.

When storing food or food preparation equipment, ensure that nothing that might drip or otherwise cause contamination is placed above it. For example, it is not acceptable to store raw meat on a shelf above knives used for chopping meat, because the raw meat may drip onto the equipment. This increases the risk of spreading pathogens.

In general, it is best to store hazardous chemicals, waste products, and other pollutants in a separate room or closet that is distant from food preparation. This reduces the risk of accidental exposure from employees passing through a room with contaminants. A designated locked janitorial closet is often the best choice for storing cleaning products and other hazardous chemicals.

## ANSI Standards and Approval Agencies

All equipment that comes into contact with food must meet the appropriate national standards as established by the National Sanitation Foundation (NSF), which is accredited by the American National Standards Institute (ANSI). Under the NSF guidelines, food service equipment must be made of nonabsorbent, corrosion resistant, smooth material. It must also be durable, easy to clean, and damage resistant. For this reason, food preparation equipment is often made of stainless steel, which meets all these criteria.

Facilities and Equipment

## Regulations and Standards

All equipment should be regularly inspected and maintained by qualified technicians. Establishing a regular maintenance schedule, both in-house and with a technician, can help to ensure that the equipment is always in top working order. In addition, any equipment that appears to be malfunctioning and/or sustains damage should be immediately checked by a qualified technician.

Cleaning stations are critical to maintaining healthy, hygienic facilities. Dishwashers should be installed in a convenient, easily reachable location and should be installed according to the manufacturer's specifications. Dishwashers should be cleaned and maintained regularly. Always use detergents that are approved by the local regulatory agencies. Ensure that the dishwasher uses suitably hot water, 165 to 180 °F depending on the machine, and has sufficient water pressure to thoroughly clean and sanitize the dishes and utensils. Suitable dishwashers should come equipped with the ability to measure water pressure and temperature as well as the concentration of cleaning and sanitizing chemical agents.

Lighting needs vary by area, but lighting should be bright enough that workers can easily see the condition of the foods and the food prep surfaces. Good lighting is also necessary to maintain cleanliness and identify areas that need maintenance. The brightness, or intensity, of lighting is measured in lux, or foot-candles. Requirements, particularly in food prep areas, are dictated by local ordinances.

Lighting should be inspected regularly. Light sources should use shatter-resistant bulbs of the correct size and luminosity and should be adequately covered to prevent broken glass contamination in the event that a bulb does break. Burnt-out bulbs should be changed immediately as needed.

Ventilation refers to the airflow of the facility. Adequate airflow is necessary to prevent the buildup of heat, smoke, steam, and condensation and to provide employees and customers with fresh air. Ventilation also helps to remove any odors or fumes from cooking, cleaning, and/or sanitization. Ventilation systems can collect a buildup from grease and other contaminants, so they should be cleaned regularly. It is also important to have ventilation systems inspected regularly by a licensed technician to ensure that there are no blockages and that the system is in optimal condition.

## Gauges and Thermometers

Currently, two types of thermometers are readily available for use in food service facilities: **digital thermometers** and **dial thermometers**. These types are organized by how the temperature is read and displayed. Both types operate by inserting the thermometer into food either during cooking or after the food is fully cooked. The metals in the thermometer warm up to the food's temperature, and then the digital screen or dial shows the temperature. How deep to insert the thermometer and how long to leave it in the food depends on the particular model. The CPFM should always refer to the

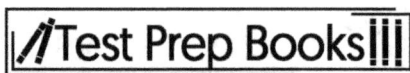

Facilities and Equipment

manufacturer's directions for correct usage. The following table notes a few common thermometer types and how they may be used.

| Thermometer | Usage |
|---|---|
| Thermocouple or thermistor thermometer | <ul><li>Quick, digital display</li><li>Sensor located in the tip of the probe</li><li>Can be used for foods of any thickness</li><li>Oven cord thermistor thermometers can be left in food during cooking</li></ul> |
| Bimetallic stemmed thermometer | <ul><li>Checks temperatures between 0°F and 220°F</li><li>Dial display</li><li>Insert up to the dimple, usually 2–3 inches</li><li>Good for larger and thicker foods</li></ul> |
| Infrared thermometer | <ul><li>Measures surface temperatures</li></ul> |
| Maximum registering thermometer | <ul><li>Displays the maximum temperature measured while being used</li></ul> |
| Time–temperature indicator (TTI) | <ul><li>Changes colors to indicate time–temperature abuse for stored food/deliveries</li></ul> |

Using thermometers is important to ensure that food has been heated enough to kill any potential pathogens. This is a heat range from 140 °F to 165 °F, depending on the type of food. To ensure that the thermometer's reading is correct, it must be calibrated. The thermometer's accuracy can be quickly tested by immersing it in a glass of ice water for at least 30 seconds. If the thermometer reads 32 °F, then it is measuring accurately. If it does not, it must be recalibrated. This can be done on most dial thermometers by turning a nut or screw placed underneath the dial. Turning this nut also turns the thermometer's pointer to the correct temperature. For other types of thermometers, the CPFM should reference the manufacturer's directions to calibrate the thermometer.

A thermometer can also be calibrated with boiling water. This follows the same process to check that the thermometer reads 212 °F.

Like other food preparation equipment, food thermometers must be sanitized after use. Do not immerse completely in water. Instead, wash carefully by hand with hot soapy water. Calibrating the thermometer should be part of the facility's daily routine. Record the results of calibration to document proof that the facility's thermometer was working appropriately. For other maintenance requirements, the CPFM should consult their thermometer's manual.

## Prevention of Cross Connection by Air Gap or Backflow Prevention

All water used in food preparation and in cleaning and sanitizing food-prep surfaces and equipment must be clean and potable, meaning that the water is suitable for drinking. City and local ordinances determine approved water sources, which usually include city-provided public water; private sources such as wells, as long as they are properly maintained and regularly inspected; enclosed, portable water containers; and water trucks. Plumbing should be installed in a way that avoids cross contamination between potable and non-potable water sources. Plumbing should be inspected regularly, and a licensed plumber should be called in immediately upon discovery of any leaks, cracks, or other issues.

Facilities and Equipment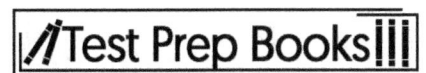

One of the biggest causes of water contamination comes from cross connections. A cross connection is when there is a physical link, such as a hose, between clean and dirty water, such as that found in drains or sewers. A hose that is attached to the faucet on a sink with the other ending resting on a drain, for example, is a contamination risk because germs and bacteria can enter the hose from the drain and work its way up through the hose to the clean faucet.

Care should also be taken to avoid cross contamination caused by backflow. Backflow occurs when there is a connection between a clean water source, such as a sink faucet, and a dirty water source, such as the water in a mop bucket. Water carrying contaminants and bacteria from the dirty water source can travel back up into the clean water source when the clean water is turned off, such as when water is siphoned from one source to another, carrying contaminants with it and thus polluting the clean water source. This is known as backsiphonage.

Backflow and cross contamination can be prevented by avoiding cross-connections. Hoses should not be attached to faucets unless the other end of the hose is held so that it does not come into contact with any unclean surface. In addition, the use of backflow prevention devices, such as vacuum breakers and reduced pressure zone backflow preventers, can help alleviate the problem. A vacuum breaker is a mechanism that closes a valve, shutting the water supply line when the water is turned off, thus preventing the dirty water from moving back up the hose. Reduced pressure zone backflow preventers have multiple check valves that seal off the water supply. Regardless of type, all backflow prevention devices must be inspected periodically by a trained technician to ensure that they are clean and in good condition. This work should be documented and kept on file by the manager.

The best way to prevent backflow is to allow for an air gap between the clean water and the dirty water. An air gap is a space between the clean water source and the potential contaminants. A properly installed sink should have an air gap between the faucet and the rim of the sink and between the drainpipe and the floor drain. This gap prevents contaminants and bacteria from being able to reach the clean water source at the faucet.

## Waste Management Practices

Garbage is a prime breeding ground for bacteria, and it is attractive to bugs, rodents, and other pests. Indoor garbage cans and containers should be waterproof, leakproof, and pest proof and should remain covered when not in use. Garbage should be removed from food prep areas as quickly as possible, and care should be taken to avoid contaminating the food prep areas in the process. Garbage cans should be cleaned regularly to avoid the buildup of contaminants that could cause illness, including wiping down the outside of the cans. Garbage cans should always be removed from the food prep areas for cleaning.

Garbage storage areas should also be well maintained. Indoors, garbage and recyclables should be kept in a designated storage area away from food storage and food prep areas. Outdoor areas should be kept clean, and storage containers, such as dumpsters, should be enclosed to prevent pest infestations. Outdoor garbage areas should also allow for suitable draining in the event of spills and rain.

The key to a clean, well-functioning facility is good maintenance practices. The entire facility should be cleaned on a regular basis. All building systems should be inspected regularly and in accordance with a regular maintenance schedule. The building should be inspected for cracks, holes, and other damaged areas that could allow for leaks and pest infestations. Pest control measures should be implemented and completed regularly. Finally, outdoor areas, including patios, parking lots, and walkways, should be kept clean, well-lit, and free of hazards. Hazardous Material

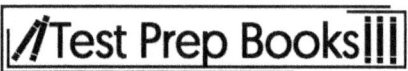

A variety of potentially hazardous chemicals are used routinely in the food service industry. Most of these chemicals are cleaning agents used to ensure proper sanitation of equipment and appliances.

All chemicals used in a food service facility must be appropriately labeled and stored. Additional information about the chemicals must be recorded on the facility's **safety data sheets** (SDS). Formerly, the SDS were called material safety data sheets (MSDS); the two have slight differences but perform the same function in the workplace. These documentation forms are required by OSHA to ensure that all employees are aware of potential hazards in the workplace.

The SDS include a variety of terms and symbols to identify a chemical's hazards. These follow an international standard for ease of use. Two signal words are used to describe the chemical: **Warning** indicates a mild hazard, while **Danger** indicates a serious hazard. However, *all* chemicals with a hazard label must be stored and used to the same standards to ensure food safety.

Each SDS also indicates what type of risk is present when using the chemical:

- **Health:** The chemical can cause harm to the employee through irritating the eyes, skin, or other parts of the body.
- **Physical:** The chemical is flammable, corrosive, or acts in another way to the detriment of the chemical's surroundings.
- **Environmental:** The chemical may react in the presence of other environmental factors, such as water or gases.

Each category has a variety of possible hazards, which are indicated by a hazard icon and described in more detail on the chemical's SDS. The CPFM is able to obtain an SDS for all chemicals used in the workplace from that chemical's manufacturer.

## Type Facility

Many systems are necessary to keep facilities operating efficiently and smoothly. Water and plumbing, lighting, ventilation, and garbage collection and disposal systems should all be well-maintained and regularly inspected. The systems must also be sufficient to meet the usage requirements for the building, including food preparation and storage as well as any customer services provided, such as dining rooms and restroom facilities.

## Approved Food Facility Materials

Flooring, walls, and ceilings should be smooth and durable for better cleaning and maintenance. Porous surfaces harbor bacteria and are much more difficult to keep clean and sanitary. Walls, floors, ceilings, and window and door surrounds should be free of cracks, gaps, holes, or other openings where pests may enter. Cracked or broken floor or ceiling tiles should be replaced immediately, both to keep pests out and to avoid a safety hazard.

Floor-mounted equipment, such as shelving, dishwashers, sinks, and counter units should be installed at least 6 inches, or 15 centimeters, off the floor to allow for proper cleaning and maintenance underneath. When the floors are cleaned and sanitized, the areas underneath this equipment should be cleaned and sanitized as well. Inspect floors regularly for damage, including inspecting underneath the equipment. Alternatively, floor-mounted equipment can be sealed to the floor to prevent contamination underneath.

Tabletop or countertop equipment must be on legs that are at least 4 inches, or 10 centimeters, high to allow for proper cleaning underneath the equipment. As with floor-mounted equipment, tabletop equipment can also be permanently affixed and sealed to the countertop.

# Integrated Pest Management

## Pests

Most common pests in food service facilities can be loosely thought of as either **rodents** or **insects**. All pests are drawn to what kitchens and other facilities provide: food, water, and shelter.

Mice and rats are common and persistent rodents. Mice are the smaller of the two, typically three or four inches in length. In contrast, a rat can easily grow to ten inches in length and weigh a pound or more. Both pests are characterized by their teeth and their droppings. A trait common to all rodents is teeth that constantly grow, requiring the animal to gnaw to keep the length manageable. Consequently, signs of chewing, tearing, or scratching in wood and plastic can indicate the presence of mice or rats. Small black droppings are also solid evidence of a rodent infestation. Mice droppings are small enough to be mistaken for dust or debris, requiring additional scrutiny. Meanwhile, rat droppings are a bit larger and less likely to be overlooked. Another important difference is that mice get most of their water through food, but rats typically require a source of standing water.

A great number of insects can plague a food service facility. The most common are:

- Cockroaches: These reddish insects are usually one to two inches long and are found in gaps or cracks in the building.

- Flies: Easy to overlook because they're so common, flies are just as able to carry illness as other insects. They're drawn to standing water and decaying material found around sources of trash or sewage.

- Ants: Small insects, typically black or red, who are drawn toward sources of food. Some bite, but typically the biggest danger is contamination of foodstuffs.

Different pests are drawn to different sources of food and water, but all find it easy to meet their needs in kitchens and other facilities. Maintaining a high standard of sanitation proactively reduces the likelihood of pests entering the facility by removing their sources of food and water.

## Pest Behaviors

All pests tend to be prey to other animals in the wild. Consequently, their behavior tends toward hiding and avoiding larger animals (such as us humans). This is also why most pests prefer to live near a source of consistent food or water. Staying near the resource allows the pest quicker access to an escape route if spotted. When searching for a pest's nest, keep a 360-degree perspective in mind. Insects can fly, and rodents are good climbers. Pests can be found in drop ceilings, burrowed into walls, underneath the floor, in drainage or sewage pipes, and other difficult-to-spot places.

Mice and cockroaches both tend to live on the building's premises, creating nests in its structure. This is why bait is often effective in addressing an infestation. Although similar to mice in many ways, rats tend to wander further in search of food, and may not actually inhabit the facility's physical location. Since the prey behavior of all three pests encourages them to avoid open spaces, a well-kept exterior reduces the odds of an infestation. Weeding, mowing, and so on deny these pests tall grasses through which to travel into the building.

# Integrated Pest Management

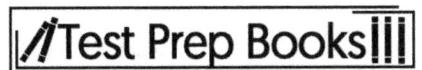

Flies and ants don't have the same claustrophobic instincts as other pests. Flies are attracted to garbage and often infest a facility's waste management before they begin to contaminate spaces that handle food directly. Sanitizing garbage cans and routinely cleaning filth off of the facility's dumpsters helps reduce the amount of decaying material available for flies to feed on. On the other hand, ants find food sources through their sense of smell. A scouting ant can lead other members of the colony to a food source, quickly infesting storage areas, kitchens, and other food handling spaces if not addressed promptly.

## Surveillance Techniques

The best pest prevention is keeping them out of the building in the first place. Carefully check all shipments for evidence of bugs or rodents. Check the truck for rodents and/or bugs, alive or dead, as well as droppings. Check the packaging for evidence of pests, such as chewed or torn packages, egg cases, droppings, or body parts. Any shipment that shows evidence of pests should be immediately refused.

## Methods to Secure Facilities Against Pests

There are three key steps to avoiding pest problems: preventing access to the facility; depriving the pests of food, water, and shelter; and working with a reputable, licensed pest control company in the event of a problem.

Pests can enter the building through cracks, vents, and other unscreened openings. Check the building thoroughly for any accessible opening. Vents should be covered with wire mesh screens that are small enough to prevent entry from even the tiniest bugs. Vents should not be covered with any solid material such as metal caps, as those can prevent necessary air flow. Cracks in walls or floors should be sealed, as should any gaps or openings around pipes, plumbing, electrical, and HVAC lines. Air curtains or fly fans should also be used in external doorways to prevent bugs from entering when the doors are open.

Pests can also be deterred by a lack of water, food, and shelter or nesting space within a building. All food should be stored in airtight containers and on shelves at least six inches off the floor or in coolers or freezers. Spills should be cleaned up immediately, and garbage should be taken outside and stored in appropriate trash containers. Garbage containers should be kept clean and tightly covered. Cleaning the entire facility regularly will eliminate food sources for pests, which will make the facility a less-desirable home for them.

## Methods to Protect Food in Storage

The easiest way for the CPFM to prevent pests from infesting a facility is to deny the pests a reason for doing so. Eliminate food sources, and you'll eliminate the pests.

Never store food on the floor, whether in a pantry, walk-in fridge, or the kitchen itself. Even if space is limited, setting food directly on the floor increases the chance that a pest will notice it. This is true for fresh food as well as prepackaged materials. For example, an inquisitive rat might gnaw on a wooden pallet on the floor, or on a cardboard box of cereal. The rat won't discover food from the former, but will from the latter.

Another important rule is to, as often as possible, keep food sealed in airtight containers. While this does prevent a pest from accessing the food, this *also* prevents pests from smelling the food. The scent

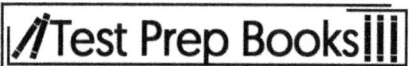

Integrated Pest Management

of food is constant around a food service facility, but sealed storage constrains those scents to during working hours when pests are less likely to explore due to humans being present. Plastic containers are effective, but glass or steel is preferable. This is because rodents are capable, over time, of gnawing through plastic. Glass or steel storage prevents this.

Finally, the CPFM ought to routinely inspect all places in which food is stored. This inspection requires not just seeking signs of pests—such as droppings or strange scents—but also physically examining the environment. Search along the edges of the space for cracks a pest might slip through. Investigate ceiling tiles, gaps around pipes, and so on. Check the sealing quality of any doors, especially on refrigerated spaces. The CPFM should inspect individual refrigerators and freezers as well as walk-in storage rooms.

## Integrated Pest Management

The key concept to pest control currently favored in the food service industry is **integrated pest management.** This perspective encourages the CPFM to view pest reduction and elimination as an ongoing process rather than an occasional task. Managing pest control is primarily about sanitation. While this may seem paradoxical at first, it makes sense considering the behavioral reasons pests infest a facility. If potential sources of food, water, and shelter are eliminated, then it's extremely unlikely that the facility will need to hire an exterminator or utilize hazardous pesticides. This both reduces expenses and improves safety.

The *management* aspect of integrated pest management is an important task for the CPFM. The CPFM is not obligated to perform all pest-prevention procedures. Rather, their task is to create a system that is appropriate for the particular facility with the result that there are fewer pests—hopefully none! Delegate weekly, monthly, and quarterly sanitation checks and pest-reduction practices. Utilize documentation to ensure that pest management is being completed. The CPFM should perform their own checks on occasion to confirm that the documentation is accurate.

## Pest Control Professionals

Even the best facilities can still sometimes experience pest problems. The smallest amount of evidence can indicate a much larger pest problem. Where there is one, there are often many. When this happens, the manager should contact a licensed, reputable pest control company immediately. A pest control company can help eliminate the pests, identify the source of the infestation, and provide additional suggestions and products to aid in prevention of future problems

## Pesticide Label Law

The use of chemicals to prevent or exterminate pests is governed by the **Federal Insecticide, Fungicide, and Rodenticide Act** (FIFRA). This act requires food service facilities to only use pesticides that have been registered as acceptable by the EPA. Under FIFRA, all registered pesticides must have a label that explains their intended purpose, how to use the pesticide appropriately, potential hazards caused by the chemical, and safety precautions, as well as basic first aid.

It's important for the CPFM to make sure they, their employees, and any contractors hired by the facility use pesticide chemicals with caution. Even when following label directions, it is possible for sprayed or dusted chemicals to contaminate food. Ensure employee safety through the use of protective equipment as described on the label, and ensure food safety by airtight sealing of any food stored in a space where chemicals will be used. If possible, temporarily move food to an alternative storage location. After chemicals have been used, thoroughly sanitize all food storage spaces and food preparation spaces to make sure the chemical does not contaminate anything that will be served to a consumer.

Always remember to check for additional regulations concerning the use of chemicals in the workplace and in food preparation within your state, city, or other local jurisdiction.

## Hazard Communication Requirements

If pesticides or other hazardous chemicals are utilized in the workplace, OSHA requires the CPFM to communicate this information to the facility's employees. The CPFM is mandated to communicate:

- List of hazardous chemicals used at the facility
- Labeling and storage of all hazardous chemicals
- Location of suitable protective equipment
- Training requirements to utilize any chemicals
- Employees who are trained and permitted to do so

These requirements protect employees and customers from harm by facilitating clear and direct communication about potential chemical risks.

Best practices when utilizing or storing hazardous chemicals recommend keeping them in a separate locked cabinet or room that only employees who have received appropriate training can access. Communicating the location and training requirement to employees reduces the risk of an untrained employee utilizing a chemical inappropriately. Likewise, communicating a label's recommended protective equipment ensures that the employees are aware of the need to use caution.

The CPFM is also required to record and document the use of hazardous chemicals in the workplace. This documentation must identify which employee used the chemicals and must specify the chemical used, where it was used, and for what purpose.

Finally, OSHA requires the CPFM to notify the USDA whenever a new chemical is introduced for use in the food service facility. Remaining in compliance with this requirement maximizes food safety and minimizes the risk to the facility's employees.

# Food Safety Regulations

## Food Safety Code

The food safety code is the set of rules made by regulatory bodies to minimize the threat of illness from food that is served to the public in commercial settings. This code includes guidelines for the handling, preparation, and storage of food. It may be implemented at the local, regional, or national level, and its purpose is to protect consumers and ensure food products meet certain safety standards.

The content of the food safety code varies depending on jurisdiction. In addition to regulations concerning food handling, preparation, and storage, the food safety code addresses topics such as proper sanitation procedures, methods to prevent foodborne illnesses, and allergen management. It also addresses the personal hygiene of food handlers and provides an outline of symptoms that must be reported by individuals working in food preparation. Those working with food must be informed as to major pathogens, toxins, and other contaminants, and know the techniques necessary to minimize the risks these pose to public health.

It is critical to follow the food safety code in order to protect the public from outbreaks of foodborne illness, particularly when working with higher risk populations, such as infants, pregnant women, the elderly, and those with pre-existing health complications.

## Health Regulatory Authority

The specifics of the food safety code for different areas are determined by their state and local health regulatory authorities. These organizations are subject to and cannot supersede the regulations set in place by national regulatory authorities, such as the Food and Drug Administration (FDA), the U.S. Department of Agriculture (USDA), the Center for Disease Control (CDC), and the U.S. Public Health Service (PHS).

State and local health regulatory authorities conduct regular inspections to ensure that every facility responsible for the preparation and service of food is following the appropriate food safety code. The timing and process of inspections, the particulars of what the inspectors look for, and the consequences of non-compliance may vary, depending on the locality.

Failure to comply with the rules and standards set by these authorities can result in a wide range of penalties. Warnings may be issued in response to small or first-time offenses, along with instructions for how to come into compliance. More serious instances of non-compliance may warrant fines or closure orders, and permits or licenses may be suspended or revoked. In egregious cases, the regulatory authority can pursue legal action against food service establishments, and the public may be notified of the establishment's violations via press release or publication on the regulatory authority's website.

## Food Safety Inspection Reports

Health regulatory authorities make food safety reports when inspecting the premises of food service establishments. Inspectors sent by these authorities are knowledgeable about food safety regulations, and they collect information to determine whether an establishment is in compliance with local rules and standards.

After completing an inspection, the inspector compiles their findings into a formal report, identifying any violations they may have observed. Once the report is compiled, it is submitted to the regulatory authority for review and provided to the food service establishment for their records. If the establishment is found to be in violation of the food safety code, the food safety inspection report will contain requirements for corrective actions and a timeline for compliance with said actions. If the establishment disagrees with the findings outlined in the report, they may have the opportunity to appeal it through a request for re-inspection or by challenging the required corrective actions.

Food safety inspection reports offer managers the opportunity to improve their establishment and create a safer environment. They may show managers areas where employees need further training, or where policy may need to be updated in order to more fully comply with the food safety code.

## Acceptable Reasons/Methods for Sampling

The acceptable reasons for sampling food products are quality control, food safety, and regulatory compliance. Sampling for quality control is generally done to ensure the food products meet the establishment's standards for taste, texture, and other sensory attributes. Food safety sampling may be done to test for the presence of pathogens, contaminants, or other potential hazards that may pose a risk to consumer health. Sampling for regulatory compliance may be done at the behest of a health regulatory authority to ensure compliance with food safety standards. Methods of sampling include:

- Random sampling—selecting samples randomly from a variety of food products
- Systematic sampling—sampling at regular intervals or according to a predetermined pattern
- Composite sampling—combining multiple samples from different locations within a batch
- Grab sampling—taking a sample from a specific point in time or location
- Split sampling—dividing a sample into smaller portions for testing by different laboratories or for different types of analysis

The method of sampling chosen depends on the reason for sampling. Random and systematic sampling tend to provide a larger picture of general quality, while grab sampling is more appropriate for quick assessments. Composite sampling offers a more representative taste of an entire batch. Split sampling is typically reserved for the type of lab testing done by regulatory authorities.

## Right to Routine Inspections

The right to routine inspections is the legal authority granted to health regulatory authorities to conduct regular inspections of food service establishments in order to ensure compliance with the food safety code. Health regulatory authorities may establish frequency or schedules based on factors such as the type of establishment, the level of risk associated with the specific food-handling activities conducted, and past compliance history. These inspections typically cover food storage, preparation, cooking methods, sanitation, and employee hygiene, among other things.

During routine inspections, health inspectors have the authority to enter food service establishments, inspect their facilities and equipment, review records and documentation, and take samples for testing.

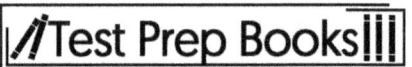

Managers and staff are legally required to cooperate with inspectors. Failure to do so can result in fines and potentially even closure orders.

If violations are noted during inspections, health regulatory authorities may issue reports identifying said violations and requiring corrective action to be taken on the part of the establishment. Establishments are legally required to comply with the directives of health regulatory authorities or else risk warnings, fines, closure orders, permit suspensions, or even legal action.

## Right to Appeal Violations

Food service establishments have the legal right to appeal findings of non-compliance asserted by health regulatory authorities. They also have the right to challenge enforcement actions or penalties which have been imposed following food safety inspections. Food service establishments have the right to due process to ensure fairness and transparency in the regulatory enforcement process.

Health regulatory authorities typically have a formal appeal process in place. They often require that an establishment submit a written appeal with evidence and documentation to support their case and attend hearings or meetings to present their arguments. Prescribed timelines associated with these proceedings must be adhered to. Grounds for appeals include disputing the accuracy of inspection findings, providing evidence of corrective actions, or challenging the interpretation or application of the food safety code.

The appeals process may result in violations being upheld, modified, or dismissed. Depending on the results, the establishment may be instructed to take further corrective action or may be granted relief from penalties. It is important for food managers to understand this process so that they can defend their legal rights and advocate for the interests of their establishment, and so that the regulatory enforcement process remains fair and transparent.

## Employee Rights of Refusal

Food service employees have the right to refuse to perform any task or activity they believe poses a risk to their health or safety. It is important for food managers to understand these rights so they can create a safe work environment for their employees.

Employees are legally protected from retaliation for exercising their right to refuse work that they reasonably believe could pose a risk of injury, illness, or harm. This means that employers may not respond to such refusal by threatening disciplinary measures such as termination.

Employers are also responsible for establishing procedures for employees to report unsafe working conditions that allow them to speak with managers or designated personnel in a timely manner. Once an employer has received such a report, they are required to investigate the matter and take appropriate actions to address the concerns raised by the employee. This involves assessing the situation and potentially implementing corrective measures to mitigate risk.

Managers have a duty to understand and protect these rights in order to create a safer working environment for employees, and to protect the establishment from legal issues that may result from violating an employee's right of refusal.

## Process to Correct Violations

The process to correct violations identified during food safety inspections conducted by health regulatory agencies is typically outlined in the food safety inspection reports provided by said agency. The inspector has undertaken the first step in identifying the violations that need to be addressed and outlining the necessary corrective actions.

Once the establishment has received the report from the health regulatory agency, they should prioritize the prescribed corrections based on the severity of risk each violation poses to food safety. Critical violations must be addressed immediately; once these have been corrected, the establishment should work on its non-critical violations. It is the manager's responsibility to put together a clear plan including objectives, timelines, and methods for verifying the necessary steps have been taken.

Once the plan is in place, the corrective actions must be implemented. These may involve re-training employees, improving sanitation procedures, repairing equipment, or making physical changes to the facility. As the corrections and changes to procedure are implemented, the manager should document them, including the specific steps taken and dates. They should collect any supporting documentation or evidence of compliance so it may be submitted to the regulatory agency. There will likely be a follow-up inspection to ensure compliance.

## SOPs for Safe Food Handling

Understanding the standard operating procedures (SOPs) for safe food handling is critical for success as a food manager. SOPs provide clear guidelines and instructions for food handlers to ensure the safety and quality of all food products. Keys SOPs to bear in mind are:

- Temperature control—keep food at temperatures below 41°F or above 135°F

- Thawing procedures—thaw foods in the refrigerator, under running cold water, or in the microwave; do NOT thaw foods at room temperature

- Storage and shelf life—use FIFO (first in, first out) rotation, monitor expiration dates, and store foods at appropriate temperatures

- Cleaning and sanitizing—use approved sanitizers, follow established cleaning schedules, and properly store cleaning tools and chemicals

- Cross-contamination—use separate cutting boards and utensils for raw and cooked foods, store raw meats below ready-to-eat foods, and clean/sanitize equipment between uses

- Allergen management—properly label allergenic ingredients, use separate equipment for allergen-free foods, and train staff on allergen awareness

- Personal hygiene—ensure requirements for handwashing, clean clothing, covering cuts or wounds, and reporting illness are being followed by employees

- Emergency procedures—have policies in place for dealing with food safety emergencies caused by issues such as power outages, equipment malfunctions, or outbreaks of foodborne illnesses

Food Safety Regulations

Awareness of these SOPs as well as any others specific to one's jurisdiction can help a manager minimize risks of foodborne illness and ensure compliance with the standards set by health regulatory agencies.

## Reportable Illnesses

Certain symptoms may indicate that an employee has an illness that may be transmitted through food. Methods of dealing with employee illness vary depending on the symptoms or pathogen involved. Reportable symptoms—those which employees must mandatorily report to management—include sore throat with fever, diarrhea, vomiting, jaundice, and lesions with pus (unless covered).

An employee with sore throat with fever may only be restricted from certain work activities unless working with high-risk populations; if they are, they should be excluded from work until symptom-free for twenty-four hours. Employees suffering from diarrhea, vomiting, or jaundice must be excluded from work and may only return after they have passed twenty-four hours symptom-free or have received medical clearance from their doctor.

A health regulatory agency must be notified if an employee is diagnosed with Salmonella, Shigella, E. coli, Hepatitis A, or Norovirus. The employee may only return to work once cleared by the regulatory authority. If an employee comes into contact with the above pathogens, they may also be excluded from work for a period specified by the health regulatory authority.

## Documentation

Documentation refers to the records, logs, and forms that food service establishments are required to maintain to demonstrate compliance with the food safety code. Copies of such documentation may be requested during inspections performed by agents of health regulatory authorities, and it is therefore essential that food managers keep fastidious records.

Documentation can include procedural information such as food safety plans, standard operating procedures, plans for handling allergens and cross-contamination, and emergency procedures for addressing food safety issues. It can also include documentation of employee training programs and certifications as well as records of supplier approvals and certificates of analysis showing supplies purchased comply with quality and safety standards. Other forms of documentation, such as temperature logs, cleaning and sanitizing logs, and complaint logs are generally updated in the regular course of business. Previous inspection reports should also be kept as a record of earlier incidences of violations, corrective actions, and follow-up activities.

Keeping these records allows food managers to ensure their establishment is complying with regulations and prevent potential issues. Understanding the purpose, content, and importance of these types of documentation is essential for food managers to maintain compliance with food safety regulations and to facilitate inspections and audits.

## Signage Requirements

Health regulatory agencies require certain signage to be posted in food service establishments in order to reinforce safe food handling practices and protect the health and wellbeing of consumers. Such signage communicates important information to employees and ensures that health and safety are kept in the forefront of the mind.

Food Safety Regulations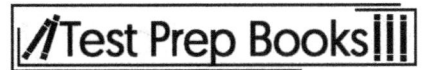

Non-smoking signs and signs reminding employees to wash their hands regularly and properly are ubiquitous examples of signage that may be required by a health regulatory authority. Procedural signage—such as those indicating proper food temperatures, food handling procedures, cleaning and sanitizing procedures, and first aid and emergency procedures are also very commonly placed in the kitchens of food service establishments. There may also be requirements for signage concerning employee illness, reminding employees of reportable symptoms as well as signs that indicate pest control measures or the presence of hazardous material.

Certain health regulatory authorities may also require signs displaying food allergy information. These inform customers as well as employees about the presence of potential allergens and concerns with cross-contamination so that consumers are better able to protect themselves.

Understanding signage requirements set by the local health regulatory authority is imperative for a food manager, as these signs help employees maintain a clean, safe, hygienic environment that customers can trust.

## Obligations to Honor Customer Contracts to Deliver Safe Food

Food service establishments have a legal and ethical responsibility to ensure that the food they serve to customers is safe for human consumption. In addition to having to follow safe food handling, preparation and storage requirements set by the local health regulatory authority, food service establishments have a legal duty of care to provide safe food that will not cause health issues if consumed. There is also an implied warranty of merchantability when any business sells a product, which means that the product sold must be fit for its intended purpose.

If there is a contract involved—as in catering agreements—there may be provisions related to food safety, quality, and the establishment's duty to abide by regulatory requirements. If these requirements are not met, customers have the right to pursue legal remedies for breach of contract. In the absence of a formal contract—as in service by a typical sit-down or fast-food restaurant—customers may still be entitled to pursue legal remedies for negligence due to the previously mentioned duty of care and implied warranty of merchantability.

Food managers must be serious about following regulations set by health regulatory authorities in all their dealings with consumers, as it is in the best interest of both the consumers and the establishment.

## Code Standards

Code standards refer to the specific requirements and guidelines set by the local health regulatory authority under the framework provided by larger agencies such as the FDA and USDA. Understanding these requirements is critical for food managers so that they can maintain a hygienic environment and ensure customer health and safety.

Code standards cover such topics as safe food handling practices, temperature control, hygiene requirements for employees, facility design, equipment standards, cleaning and sanitizing procedures, pest control, and employee training. They may vary between jurisdictions, so it is important to be familiar with the standards set by the local health regulatory authority.

These standards are updated and revised over time, so food managers must stay informed. These changes can be due to advancements in food safety science, changes in regulatory requirements,

emerging risks, and the evolution of best practices in the food industry. Regulatory authorities often provide educational resources and training materials to help managers stay current.

Failure to comply with code requirements may result in penalties such as warnings, fines, closure notices, revocation of permits and licenses, or even legal action. It is essential for food managers to take care to uphold current food standards in order to protect the customers and the food service establishment.

## Hazard Communication Requirements

Hazard communication requirements refer to an employer's obligation to ensure that employees are informed about the presence of hazardous chemicals in the workplace and trained to minimize the risk of working with such substances. Employees must be trained on safe handling practices, proper use of personal protective equipment, and emergency procedures. These requirements are in place to protect employees, prevent accidents, and facilitate emergency responses in the event of chemical spills or exposures.

Employers are required to keep an inventory of all potentially hazardous chemicals in the workplace and make sure they are properly labeled with information about their hazards and safe handling practices. Manufacturers and distributors of hazardous chemicals are required to provide Safety Data Sheets (SDS) for each chemical they produce or distribute. These forms must include detailed information about the chemical composition, physical properties, health hazards, safety precautions, and emergency procedures related to the chemical.

Employees must have access to the SDS and must be trained on how to interpret it. Employers should ensure that employees understand the hazards associated with the chemicals they are required to work with. These requirements reduce the likelihood of chemical-related accidents and injuries and promote a safe and healthy work environment.

## Employee Privacy of Personnel and Health Records

Employee privacy is protected by various laws and regulations, and food managers must understand and comply with these in order to protect the confidentiality of employee information. Employers may only collect employee personnel and health information for legitimate business purposes, such as payroll, benefits management, performance evaluation, disciplinary action, and compliance with legal requirements.

Employers are responsible for protecting employee information from unauthorized access, disclosure, alteration, or destruction, utilizing methods such as encryption, password protection, secure storage, and access control. Access to employee information should be restricted to authorized individuals with a legitimate need to know the specific information disclosed. Individuals with access to sensitive employee information should be trained in the importance of employee privacy and their responsibilities in safeguarding this privacy. Training should include information on data security, confidentiality obligations, and compliance with privacy laws.

Employers should have established policies and procedures for the retention and disposal of employee information. Records should be retained as long as they are relevant and necessary and should be disposed of when no longer needed. It is important for food managers to understand and follow their legal obligations concerning employee privacy to protect the company, the employees, and themselves.

Food Safety Regulations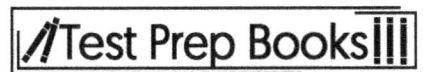

## HACCP Plan Requirement

The Hazard Analysis and Critical Control Points (HACCP) plan is a systematic approach to food safety management that is used to prevent, eliminate, or reduce safety hazards throughout the food production process. HACCP programs are mandatory and regulated by the FDA and USDA. The seven steps of an HACCP plan are:

- Conduct an analysis to identify potential hazards.
- Find critical control points (CCP) where the potential hazards can be eliminated or reduced.
- Figure out minimum and maximum limits for each critical control point.
- Establish monitoring procedures to ensure minimum and/or maximum limits for each CCP are being met.
- Establish corrective actions to take when critical limits are not met.
- Establish verification procedures to ensure the HACCP plan is working.
- Establish and maintain procedures for record-keeping and documentation.

Critical control points are specific times in the food production process where hazards are likely to occur, and measures can be instituted to reduce or eliminate the threat of these hazards. Critical limits are the minimum or maximum values that must be met at each CCP to ensure food safety (e.g., temperatures required to be maintained to prevent bacterial growth in food products). Corrective actions may include discarding food product, investigating the root causes of the failure, improving procedures, or notifying management. Documentation is important, as it demonstrates compliance with the regulations set in place by health regulatory authorities.

# Practice Test #1

1. Dishwashers should use hot water that is within what temperature range?
    a. 150 to 165 °F
    b. 155 to 170 °F
    c. 175 to 190 °F
    d. 165 to 180 °F

2. Which of the following is an alternative to elevating floor- or table-mounted equipment?
    a. Setting directly on the floor without mounting so that it can be moved easily
    b. Putting the equipment on rubber feet to prevent sliding or movement
    c. Affixing and sealing the equipment to the surface
    d. None; the equipment must be elevated in all cases

3. What is the minimum internal temperature that ground beef must be cooked to in order to be safe for consumption?
    a. 165 °F for 17 seconds
    b. 145 °F for 17 seconds
    c. 160 °F for 17 seconds
    d. 155 °F for 17 seconds

4. What temperature should the water be when mixing a chemical sanitizer?
    a. 50 °F – 75 °F
    b. 100 °F – 120 °F
    c. 75 °F – 105 °F
    d. 68 °F – 100 °F

5. What temperature range listed is the *temperature danger zone*?
    a. 41 °F – 135 °F
    b. 41 °F – 138 °F
    c. 40 °F – 140 °F
    d. 45 °F – 140 °F

6. Which of the following is NOT a suitable hand-drying option in handwashing stations?
    a. Clean hand towel
    b. Paper towels
    c. Continuous towel system
    d. Air dryer

7. What is the accrediting agency for the NSF?
    a. FDA
    b. ANSI
    c. USDA
    d. CDC

8. How should egg dishes be prepared to be safe for consumption if they require the egg to be not fully cooked or raw?
    a. Egg dishes that require the egg to be raw or not fully cooked should be cooked to at least 145 °F.
    b. Dishes that require eggs to be not fully cooked or raw should be prepared with eggs treated for pasteurization.
    c. Egg dishes with raw egg should be cooked until the yolks are firm, though the whites can be runny.
    d. There are no special considerations that need to be made for egg dishes with raw egg since eggs are not a risk for illness.

9. What are the proper steps for cleansing and sanitizing a surface that will be used for food?
    a. Remove excess food, clean the surface with cleaning solution, rinse, apply sanitizing solution with a reusable cloth, and air dry for at least one minute.
    b. Remove excess food, clean the surface with cleaning solution, rinse, apply sanitizing solution with a disposable wipe, and air dry for at least one minute.
    c. Clean the surface with a cleaning solution that removes excess food, rinse, apply sanitizing solution with a disposable wipe, and air dry for at least one minute.
    d. Remove excess food, clean the surface with cleaning solution, rinse, apply sanitizing solution with a disposable wipe, and wipe dry.

10. Which of the following is NOT a requirement for the construction material for food service equipment?
    a. Corrosion resistant
    b. Nonabsorbent
    c. Stainless steel
    d. Smooth

11. Which of the following groups is NOT considered a highly susceptible population (HSP)?
    a. Children under five
    b. People experiencing poverty
    c. People with kidney disease
    d. Older adults

12. Which of the following is the safest way to thaw frozen meat?
    a. Setting the frozen meat down on a counter to allow it to thaw to room temperature
    b. Placing the frozen meat in a sink full of hot water
    c. Thawing frozen meat in the microwave and then placing it in the refrigerator for later use
    d. Moving the frozen meat into the refrigerator

13. Meredith needs to sanitize the restaurant's utensils after the lunch rush. What is the best method to use?
    a. Clean them in soapy water and rinse well
    b. Soak them in very hot water
    c. Spray them with a quaternary ammonium compound
    d. Wipe them down with a clean towel

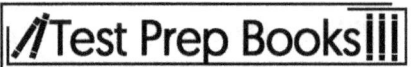

14. Which statement is most accurate regarding food contamination?
    a. Food that is properly wrapped or stored in a container is unlikely to become contaminated.
    b. Once food is placed in a buffet serving area, food employees have no control over the risk of contamination.
    c. Food employees are unable to control risks from contamination that occurs before food arrives at the facility.
    d. The risk of contamination can be decreased by sending sick employees home.

15. The Sunday Brunch Spot is having their kitchen remodeled. The construction contractor has recommended using a textured spray on the walls to help hide any defects in the new drywall before painting, but per the owner's request, he has made several options available. Which option would be the best choice?
    a. Go with the textured spray; the contractor is the expert here.
    b. Choose a smooth, durable surface, such as wall tiles.
    c. Do the textured spray, but make sure the paint is washable.
    d. Request a smooth drywall finish with durable, washable paint.

16. Aflatoxin is commonly found in which of these foods?
    a. Fish
    b. Tomatoes
    c. Nuts
    d. Eggs

17. How often should machines that hold and/or dispense TCS foods be cleaned?
    a. Twice daily
    b. Daily
    c. Twice weekly
    d. Weekly

18. If a can of green beans is at the room temperature of 67 °F before and after opening, what is the maximum amount of time the green beans can remain at this room temperature before being consumed or discarded?
    a. 2 hours
    b. 4 hours
    c. 6 hours
    d. They cannot be held at this temperature.

19. What is the level of acidity or alkalinity in the water called?
    a. pH
    b. Hardness
    c. Buffering capacity
    d. Salinity

20. Which of the following is NOT a time when food contact surfaces should be cleaned and sanitized?
    a. After use
    b. When changing to prepare a new kind of food
    c. Whenever a task is interrupted and contamination may have occurred
    d. Every six hours during continuous use

21. Which term refers to the removal of dirt and debris, such as food particles, from a surface?
    a. Sanitizing
    b. Disinfecting
    c. Cleaning
    d. Polishing

22. Which method would be most effective for preventing Scromboid poisoning due to fish?
    a. Ensure fish are kept at or below 41 °F beginning as soon as possible after being caught or harvested.
    b. Ensure fish are not caught from bodies of water with high histamine concentrations.
    c. Cook fish to an internal temperature of at least 145 °F for at least 15 seconds.
    d. Avoid fish with an unusual appearance, smell, or taste.

23. What does NSF stand for?
    a. National Sanitation Foundation
    b. Nationwide Safety Foundation
    c. National Safety Federation
    d. Nationwide Standard for Foods

24. What is the general prescribed time range to allow a chemical sanitizer that contains chlorine to remain on a surface?
    a. At least seven seconds
    b. At least sixty seconds
    c. At least thirty seconds
    d. At least ten seconds

25. How should the strength of chemical sanitizer be checked?
    a. Measuring the temperature
    b. Reading the label on the package
    c. Using a test kit
    d. Mixing one-part chemical to one-part water

26. What causes glassware to experience thermal shock?
    a. Glass moving quickly from very cold to very hot
    b. Glasses being stacked on top of one another
    c. Glasses hitting each other while soaking in a sink
    d. A glass reaching room temperature before being run in the dishwasher

27. Under what conditions would it be acceptable to use a cutting board to cut fish after using it to cut chicken?
    a. When the cutting board is turned over after cutting the chicken so that the clean side is used for the fish
    b. When a separate set of single-use gloves is used with each item
    c. When the chicken and fish will be combined for cooking as part of the same dish
    d. When there is no risk that the customer ordering the fish is allergic to chicken

28. What is the minimum temperature that a brined ham must be cooked to in order to be safe for consumption?
    a. 140 °F
    b. 145 °F
    c. 155 °F
    d. 160 °F

29. Jane is a manager at the Silver House restaurant. Lately, the restaurant's produce supplier has not been meeting its the needs, and Jane would like to change suppliers. One of the waitstaff has a cousin who is a farmer and farm-to-table supplier who might be able to take over. Who can Jane contact to see if this new supplier has undergone inspections?
    a. FDA or HACCP
    b. FDA or USDA
    c. USDA or HACCP
    d. HACCP or GMP

30. What information should be included in a supplier's safety inspection report?
    a. Receiving, storage, and processing practices
    b. Staff training and diversity
    c. Types of food products provided by the supplier
    d. Geographical range of the supplier's delivery route

31. In a three-compartment sink, what minimum temperature should the water be in the cleaning and rinsing compartments?
    a. 100 °F
    b. 110 °F
    c. 105 °F
    d. 115 °F

32. Which of the following is NOT a requirement for commercial dishwashers?
    a. Ability to measure temperature
    b. Ability to be pre-programmed to run on schedule
    c. Ability to measure water pressure
    d. Ability to measure concentration of cleaning agents

33. What does HACCP stand for?
    a. Healthy Analysis Critical Control Points
    b. Hazard Analysis Critical Control Points
    c. Hazard and Consumer Control Points
    d. Health and Consumer Care Points

34. What is the term used for disease-causing microorganisms such as bacteria, viruses, parasites, and fungi?
    a. Pathogens
    b. Infections
    c. Contaminants
    d. Diagnoses

35. When receiving a delivery, a visual inspection should include which of the following?
    a. The purchase order
    b. The delivery driver
    c. The outside of the delivery truck
    d. The inside of the delivery truck

36. Which of the following is the proper way to store food?
    a. Foods can be held within the temperature danger zone if they are not held there for too long.
    b. Old foods should be stored behind newer foods.
    c. So long as foods are kept out of the temperature danger zone, there is no specific way they need to be stored.
    d. Raw foods should be stored away from and below ready-to-eat foods to prevent cross-contamination.

37. What is the proper way to hold food that is being marinated?
    a. When food is being marinated, it should be held in the fridge.
    b. Food being marinated can be held at or below room temperature.
    c. Food should only be marinated in the freezer.
    d. If a marinade has been boiled, the temperature it is held at does not matter.

38. Which of the following is one of the CDC's five foodborne illness risk factors?
    a. Inadequate employee training
    b. Improper hand washing
    c. Improper holding times and temperatures
    d. Fecal contamination

39. How should fresh meat and poultry be temperature checked?
    a. By inserting a thermometer directly into the thickest part of the meat
    b. By inserting a thermometer directly into the thinnest part of the meat
    c. By placing the thermometer between two pieces of meat
    d. By folding the meat around the thermometer

40. At what temperature should cold foods, such as meats, be delivered?
    a. 35 °F or cooler
    b. 41 °F or cooler
    c. 45 °F or cooler
    d. 47 °F or cooler

41. What is the longest amount of time that fresh shellfish can be frozen?
    a. Six months
    b. Nine months
    c. Twelve months
    d. Eighteen months

42. Which list includes each of the major food allergens?
    a. Meat, poultry, eggs, raw milk products, seafood, and raw vegetables, grains, and fruits
    b. Peanuts, tree nuts, sesame, eggs, crustacean shellfish, wheat, milk, soybeans, and fish
    c. Gluten, latex, leafy greens, sprouts, raw flour, dairy, nuts, seeds, and refined sugar
    d. Tuna fish, tofu, cashew nuts, deviled eggs, lobster, couscous, soft cheeses, and hummus

43. Which of the following is NOT an example of a TCS food?
    a. Milk
    b. Cut melon
    c. Eggs
    d. Uncooked beans

44. Which of these is an example of physical contamination?
    a. Particles of insulation that fell into an open bag of oats from a ceiling repair
    b. *Shigella* bacteria from a food worker who did not practice proper glove use contaminating pasta salad
    c. High levels of mercury in rice that was treated with a mercury-based fungicide
    d. Ciguatoxin present in snapper caught in Florida

45. Toxoplasmosis would best be classified as which of the following?
    a. A foodborne infection
    b. A physical hazard
    c. A rare condition
    d. A developing-world illness

46. Which of the following is an example of a sanitary personal hygiene practice?
    a. Washing hands in warm soapy water for at least twenty seconds
    b. An employee handling food wearing a few rings on their hands
    c. Hair not being contained by a hair restraint while preparing food
    d. An employee keeping their food near where food is being prepared for customers

47. If a customer has food allergies and has requested that their meal be free of the nine major food allergens, which action would be recommended for protecting the customer?
    a. Rinse off uncooked chicken that was stored with shrimp and fish before cooking it for the customer.
    b. Prepare the meal in a separate area with freshly cleaned and sanitized equipment.
    c. Ensure that eggs and milk products used as ingredients are pasteurized and thoroughly cooked.
    d. Pick out all nuts on a premade salad before serving it to the customer.

48. Which of these symptoms would most likely indicate that a customer is having a food allergy reaction?
    a. Jaundice
    b. Tingling around the mouth
    c. Difficulty breathing
    d. Weight loss

49. What minimum internal temperature must eggs that will be hot-held for service be cooked to?
    a. 145 °F
    b. 150 °F
    c. 155 °F
    d. 160 °F

50. When inspecting for possible entry points for pests, which of the following areas should be checked?
    a. Cracks, gaps, and holes in walls, floors, ceilings, and window and door surrounds
    b. Openings between shelves in dry storage
    c. Underneath equipment, counters, and tables
    d. Inside cooler and freezer units and in and around stoves and ovens

51. Michelle accepted an order of shucked shellfish that was at a temperature of 44 °F. The driver told her he had been on the road for three hours already that morning. Michelle put the shellfish in the refrigerator within an hour. Five hours later, she checked the shellfish and found the temperature to be 42 degrees. Can the chefs begin using this shellfish for the evening menu?
    a. Yes, the shellfish was delivered at an appropriate temperature.
    b. Yes, the shellfish was put into the refrigerator within an hour of delivery.
    c. No, the shellfish did not cool to a sufficient temperature within the prescribed time frame.
    d. No, the shellfish should not have been on the truck for so long.

52. Which of the following is a sign that a frozen food is potentially unsafe to keep for consumption due to thawing and refreezing upon arriving in a shipment?
    a. The packaging is broken open.
    b. There are ice crystals on the packaging.
    c. The packaging is bloated.
    d. The frozen food is discolored.

53. Concerning bacterial contamination, which of these is a true statement?
    a. Bacteria grow only in the danger zone.
    b. Certain bacteria produce toxins.
    c. Proper cooking will kill all bacteria.
    d. Bacterial infections result in immediate symptoms.

54. If a pan of lasagna is removed from cooking at 375 °F and must be cooled and refrigerated, what is the maximum amount of time the lasagna itself, as measured by a food thermometer, can safely remain in the danger zone temperature range?
    a. 2 hours
    b. 4 hours
    c. 6 hours
    d. 8 hours

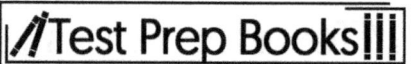

55. Which of the following is the proper way to prepare produce for consumption?
    a. Inspect, throw out rotten produce and remove damaged parts, rinse thoroughly (even if the skin or rind is not eaten), cut
    b. Inspect, throw out rotten produce and remove damaged parts, rinse thoroughly (unless the skin or rind is not going to be eaten), cut
    c. Rinse thoroughly (even if skin or rind is not eaten), cut, throw out rotten produce, remove damaged parts
    d. Inspect, throw out rotten produce and remove damaged parts, rinse thoroughly with soap (even if the skin or rind is not eaten), cut

56. Which of these is the leading cause of foodborne illness in the United States?
    a. *E. coli*
    b. *Salmonella*
    c. Mold
    d. Norovirus

57. Hepatitis A is an example of what type of pathogen?
    a. Bacterium
    b. Parasite
    c. Virus
    d. Fungus

58. What is the minimum internal temperature that raw poultry must be cooked to?
    a. 145 °F
    b. 150 °F
    c. 160 °F
    d. 165 °F

59. Which publication contains the Good Agricultural Practices (GAP) guidelines for growing produce?
    a. *Food Code*
    b. *Dietary Guidelines for Americans*
    c. *Guidance for Industry: Guide to Minimize Microbial Food Safety Hazards for Fresh Fruits and Vegetables*
    d. *Foreign Supplier Verification Programs for Importers of Food for Humans and Animals*

60. Which term best describes an illness caused by the presence of too much copper in spaghetti sauce that was stored in a copper pan?
    a. Foodborne infection
    b. Foodborne intoxication
    c. Foodborne illness due to physical contamination
    d. Scombroid poisoning

61. A pork roast must be cooked to what minimum internal temperature?
    a. 140 °F
    b. 145 °F
    c. 150 °F
    d. 155 °F

62. Belinda's manager has asked her to receive the order of meat from the supplier. What equipment and information does Belinda need to have to properly receive and inspect the delivery?
   a. Purchase order and thermometer
   b. Thermometer and scale
   c. Purchase order and tape measure
   d. Tape measure and scale

63. Manuel has a new dry goods supplier who would like to schedule a delivery for before the restaurant opens in the morning, when no staff or management would be available to receive the delivery. Should Manuel permit this?
   a. No, management or staff should always be available to receive the delivery.
   b. Yes, this is called a key drop delivery and is fine.
   c. No, a key drop delivery should only be permitted by well-known, trusted suppliers.
   d. Yes, the delivery driver can leave the goods just outside the back door of the restaurant.

64. What is the recommended maximum amount of time that lamb chops can be safely stored in the refrigerator?
   a. Two to four days
   b. One to two days
   c. Three to four days
   d. Three to five days

65. What is the proper temperature for hot-held food to be kept at?
   a. 140 °F and above
   b. 135 °F and above
   c. 138 °F and above
   d. 145 °F and above

66. What is one step that can be taken to address one of the five most common foodborne illness risk factors?
   a. Conduct periodic visual inspections of the interior of randomly selected raw animal products to ensure they are not contaminated with toxins or pathogens.
   b. Post signage in dining areas warning customers of the dangers of sharing utensils, cups, and straws.
   c. Train employees on proper hand washing and its importance for preventing foodborne illnesses.
   d. Avoid using equipment that contains glass that could break, such as glass thermometers that are not covered with a shatterproof coating.

67. Other than temperature, what is one way to tell that eggs have been fully cooked?
   a. The whites and yolks are both firm.
   b. The whites are firm.
   c. The yolks are firm.
   d. The whites and yolks are partially firm.

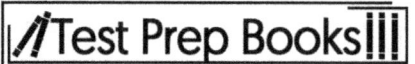

68. Which of the following is the proper practice to replace old food in a self-service bar?
    a. The container of old food should be replaced with an entirely new container of food, which should be covered as it is brought from the kitchen to the self-serve area.
    b. So long as the temperature is held above 135 °F, new food can be added to old food after being brought out from the kitchen to the self-serve area.
    c. The container of old food should be removed and replaced with a container of new food and does not need to be covered on its way to the self-serve area.
    d. Old food should be removed from the container, after which new food can be placed into the container.

69. How often should floors beneath floor-mounted equipment be cleaned and inspected?
    a. Every time the rest of the floor is cleaned
    b. Every two days
    c. Weekly
    d. At the end of each shift

70. In the United States, about how many people become sick with foodborne illnesses each year?
    a. 128,000
    b. One in six
    c. Three thousand
    d. 10 percent

71. Which of the following is a symptom of a potential foodborne illness?
    a. Shivering
    b. Sore throat
    c. Headache
    d. Fever

72. An employee reports to work at a meat packing plant with an open wound. Under which of the following circumstances are they allowed to work?
    a. If they loosely wrap the wound with cloth
    b. If they completely cover the wound with a bandage
    c. If the wound is not leaking blood
    d. If the wound is not visibly infected

73. The Occupational Safety and Health Administration (OSHA) requires the CPFM to communicate which of the following to their employees?
    a. The report of any pests spotted in the facility
    b. The training requirements to use pesticides in day-to-day operations
    c. The list of employees not permitted to use hazardous chemicals
    d. The dates on which the CPFM will inspect the facility

74. Which of the following risks of pest infestations is NOT reduced by appropriate integrated pest management practices?
    a. Food sources
    b. Water sources
    c. Access to the building
    d. Sources of shelter

75. A CPFM finds a plastic storage bin that has a jagged hole in it, through which a pest has been eating the dry goods that were stored inside. The bin was stored on the floor. The storage room has no strange odors or signs of a nest. Which of the following pests is most likely infesting the facility?
   a. Mice
   b. Cockroaches
   c. Flies
   d. Squirrels

76. Which of the following is the best way to prevent cockroaches from infesting a food service facility?
   a. Make sure the garbage bins are cleaned regularly.
   b. Seal any cracks in the wall or ceiling promptly.
   c. Keep walk-in refrigerators at 40 °F or below.
   d. Avoid placing food storage bins on the floor.

77. A CPFM hires an exterminator to end an infestation of mice. The exterminator uses an approved spray to poison potential nests and leaves poisoned bait and traps. What should be done before the facility can use the treated spaces to prepare food?
   a. Inspect the facility to ensure that pest management practices are being followed.
   b. Clean other rooms to confirm that the mice did not spread during extermination.
   c. Sanitize the treated rooms to avoid chemicals contaminating any food.
   d. Train the employees on how to use the exterminator's chemicals in case the exterminator returns.

78. Who determines the specifics of the food safety code for individual jurisdictions?
   a. The FDA
   b. The USDA
   c. State and local regulatory authorities
   d. The CDC

79. Health regulatory authorities often send agents to food service establishments. What is the purpose of these visits?
   a. To inspect the establishment, create a report of violations, and recommend corrective measures
   b. To perform routine maintenance on kitchen equipment and ensure that it is working properly
   c. To educate the staff on new food preparation and cooking techniques
   d. To interview customers and put together a report of consumer complaints

80. Which of the following is NOT an acceptable reason for sampling food product?
   a. To ensure food products meet the establishment's standards
   b. To inform an employee about the flavor of a certain dish
   c. To test for the presence of pathogens or other contaminants
   d. Because a health regulatory agency ordered the sampling

# Answer Explanations #1

**1. D:** Dishwashers should use water that is between 165 and 180 °F. Any cooler, Choices A and B, and the water will not sufficiently kill germs and bacteria. Any hotter, Choice C, and the water could damage the equipment.

**2. C:** Floor- and table-mounted equipment can be affixed directly to the surface and sealed instead of elevating it. Putting the equipment directly on the floor, Choice A, or on rubber feet, Choice B, is not sufficient. While elevating the equipment is common, it is not the only option, as in Choice D.

**3. D:** Choice D correctly states that the minimum internal temperature that ground beef must be cooked to for safety is 155 °F for at least 17 seconds. Choices A, B, and D are incorrect as 165 °F, 145 °F, and 155 °F are not the minimum internal temperature that ground beef must reach.

**4. D:** When mixing a chemical sanitizer, the water temperature should be between 68 and 100 °F, depending on which chemical is being used. Choices A, B, and C are incorrect.

**5. A:** Choice A states the correct temperature danger zone: 41 °F–135 °F. Choices A, B, and D are incorrect because they do not list the correct temperature ranges of the temperature danger zone.

**6. A:** Reusable towels, such as traditional hand towels, can hold bacteria and are not suitable for commercial handwashing stations. Choices B, C, and D are better options.

**7. B:** The NSF is overseen by the American National Standards Institute (ANSI). The FDA, Choice A, and the USDA, Choice C, are both regulatory agencies for food safety. The CDC, Choice D, is the Centers for Disease Control.

**8. B:** Dishes that require raw or not fully cooked eggs should be prepared with eggs that have been pasteurized. Choice A is incorrect as there is not a temperature that these dishes must be cooked to; rather, they should be made with treated eggs. Choice C is incorrect as in egg dishes with raw egg, neither part of the egg will be firm. Also, pasteurized eggs should be used in this scenario. Choice D is incorrect as eggs are a risk for illness, and there are considerations to make for dishes that use raw or not fully cooked eggs.

**9. B:** Choice B states the correct steps. First, the surface is cleared of excess food before a cleaning solution is used to clean the surface. The cleaning solution is then rinsed, and the sanitizing solution is applied, which then air dries for at least one minute. Choice A is incorrect because it states that the sanitizing solution should be applied with a reusable cloth rather than a disposable one. Choice C is incorrect because it states that the cleaning solution removes the excess food. However, excess food should be removed before the cleaning solution is used. Choice D is incorrect; it states that the surface should be wiped dry after using the sanitizing solution, not air dried.

**10. C:** While stainless steel is not a requirement for food service equipment, it is a popular choice because it is corrosion resistant, Choice A, nonabsorbent, Choice B, and smooth, Choice D.

**11. B:** Apart from other risk factors that would classify them as part of a highly susceptible population (HSP), people experiencing poverty are not considered an HSP. Choice A is incorrect because children under five are considered preschool-aged children and are an HSP because their immune systems have

Answer Explanations #1

not yet fully developed. Choice C is incorrect because people who have kidney disease or other diseases that weaken the immune system are considered immunocompromised people, making them part of that HSP. Choice D is incorrect because older adults are considered an HSP.

**12. D:** Choice D states one of the safe ways to thaw food of the three provided in the text. Choice A is incorrect as food should not be left to thaw at room temperature. Choice B is incorrect as food should be thawed in cold water, not hot water. Choice C is incorrect; while food can be thawed in the microwave, it is safest if it is cooked immediately following thawing.

**13. B:** Heat sanitization, submerging the utensils in water that is at least 171 °F and soaking them for at least thirty seconds, is the best choice here. Cleaning the utensils with soapy water, Choice A, is good to remove any food debris but will not sanitize them. Using a chemical sanitizer, such as a quaternary ammonium compound in Choice C, is good for food prep surfaces, but it is not an ideal choice for small items like utensils. Simply wiping with a towel, Choice D, will not sufficiently clean nor sanitize the utensils.

**14. D:** Sick employees are more likely to be contagious and contaminate food with pathogens, so excluding them from work will help reduce the risk of biological contamination of food. Choice A is incorrect because wrapping or enclosing time/temperature control for safety (TCS) foods will not protect them from becoming contaminated by overgrowth of pathogens through time and temperature abuse. Choice B is incorrect because there are still important steps that food employees can and should take to control the risk of contamination, such as ensuring food is shielded from overhead and maintained at a proper temperature and providing appropriate utensils to serve food and clean plates for customers making return trips to the buffet. Choice C is incorrect because there are important steps that food employees can and should take to control risks associated with contamination that occurs before food arrives at a facility, including ensuring that food is only received from approved facilities and that it is received at a proper temperature.

**15. B:** Walls in food service facilities should be smooth, durable, and easy to clean. In the case of a kitchen area, wall tiles would be the best choice. Choices A, C, and D all allow for a more porous surface, which can harbor bacteria.

**16. C:** Aflatoxin is a mycotoxin produced by some types of *Aspergillus* molds. It grows naturally on some crops, especially grains and nuts, and can be found in the milk of cows that eat contaminated grains. Choices A, B, and D are incorrect because fish, tomatoes, and eggs are not as likely to be contaminated with aflatoxin.

**17. B:** Machines that hold and/or dispense TCS foods should be cleaned daily according to the manufacturer's directions and local regulations. Choices A, C, and D are incorrect.

**18. B:** Because the temperature of the green beans is at or below 70 °F when they become a TCS food (when the can is opened) and during the holding time, the maximum amount of time they can be held without temperature control is 4 hours. Choice A is incorrect because, as long as their temperature remains at or below 70 °F, the green beans do not need to be used or discarded this quickly. Choice C is incorrect because 6 hours is too long to hold a TCS food without temperature control unless the food starts out at or below 41 °F and remains at or below 70 °F for the duration of the time. Choice D is incorrect because canned green beans can be held at 67 °F as long as they are properly labeled and consumed or discarded within 4 hours.

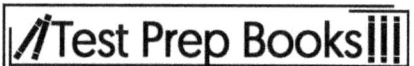

Answer Explanations #1

**19. A:** The level of acidity in water is its pH level. Water hardness, Choice *B*, refers to the level of minerals in the water. Buffering capacity, Choice *C*, is the water's ability to maintain a stable pH. Choice *D* refers to the number of dissolved substances in the water.

**20. D:** Food contact surfaces should be cleaned and sanitized every four hours during continuous use, as well as at all the times listed in Choices *A*, *B*, and *C*.

**21. C:** *Cleaning* is the removal of dirt and debris from surfaces. *Sanitizing*, Choice *A*, is the removal of bacteria, and *disinfecting*, Choice *B*, removes bacteria and viruses. *Polishing*, Choice *D*, generally refers to the appearance of a surface rather than its cleanliness.

**22. A:** Scromboid poisoning is an overdevelopment of histamine that occurs after fish are harvested and can be prevented by holding fish under refrigeration temperatures. Choice *B* is incorrect because, unlike other fish toxins, the histamine toxin does not accumulate from the fish's environment and food sources. Choice *C* is incorrect because, although it is important to cook fish to an internal temperature of 145 °F for at least 15 seconds, freezing and cooking do not inactivate fish toxins. Choice *D* is incorrect because, although histamine toxins can sometimes cause the fish to have an unusual appearance, smell, or taste, this is not a reliable indicator of whether the toxins are present.

**23. A:** The NSF is the National Sanitation Foundation, the agency responsible for establishing the standards for food preparation equipment. Choices *B*, *C*, and *D* are made-up answers.

**24. C:** The manufacturer's instructions will give specific information, but generally, sanitizer that contains chlorine should remain on the surface for at least thirty seconds. Choices *A*, *B*, and *D* are incorrect.

**25. C:** The concentration of chemical sanitizer should be checked using a test kit, which is often included with the product. The test kit helps ensure that the mixture contains the right amount of chemical mixed with the right amount of water. While the temperature of the water, Choice *A*, is important, that does not help to measure concentration. Similarly, the label on the package, Choice *B*, will instruct as to the appropriate concentration to use, but reading the label will not measure the mixture itself. The appropriate mixture should be prepared according to the label instructions, not simply by using equal measures as in Choice *D*.

**26. A:** Choice *A* is correct as thermal shock is caused when a glass moves too quickly from one extreme temperature to another. Choice *B* is incorrect; while glasses should not be stacked on top of one another, this is not a cause of thermal shock. Choice *C* is incorrect; glasses should not be allowed to make contact in this way, but glasses hitting one another while soaking in a sink is not a cause of thermal shock. Choice *D* is incorrect because glass should be allowed to reach room temperature before being run in the dishwasher; this prevents thermal shock from occurring.

**27. C:** Because the cooking temperature for fish is lower than the cooking temperature for chicken, no equipment or utensils should be used with fish after being used with raw chicken without first being washed and sanitized unless the fish and chicken will be cooked together as part of the same dish. Choice *A* is incorrect because turning over a cutting board does not prevent cross-contamination. Choice *B* is incorrect because cross-contamination would occur from the cutting board regardless of whether clean gloves are used with the fish. Choice *D* is incorrect because the risk of cross-contamination from chicken to fish involves pathogens that can affect anyone, regardless of whether they have food allergies.

Answer Explanations #1

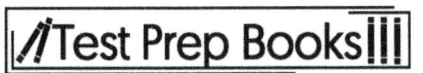

**28. C:** Choice C is correct, as mechanically tenderized meat like a brined ham must be cooked to a minimum temperature of 155 °F for at least 17 seconds. Choices A, B, and D list incorrect cooking temperatures for a brined ham.

**29. B:** The inspection reports for suppliers can be found by contacting either the US Food and Drug Administration (FDA) or the US Department of Agriculture (USDA). The HACCP, the Hazard Analysis Critical Control Points, Choices A and C, is a food safety management system, and GMPs, Choice D, are Good Manufacturing Practices.

**30. A:** A safety inspection report should include the supplier's receiving, storage, and processing practices. While staff training should be included, Choice B, the diversity of the staff is irrelevant to a safety inspection report. The report does not typically include information about specific products, Choice C, or delivery routes, Choice D.

**31. B:** Choice B is correct as the minimum temperature that the water of the cleansing and rinsing compartments of the three-compartment sink should be is 110 °F. The other choices are incorrect as they are not the minimum temperature that the water of a three-compartment sink must be.

**32. B:** Dishwashers do not need to be pre-programmed, though they should be able to measure water temperature, pressure, and the concentration of cleaning agents, Choices A, C, and D.

**33. B:** HACCP is the acronym for the Hazard Analysis Critical Control Points, a food safety management system. Choices A, C, and D are made-up answers.

**34. A:** Pathogens are microorganisms that cause disease. Choice B is incorrect because the word *infection* refers to the process in which microorganisms enter the body. It would be correct to say that a pathogen has infected a person or that a person has become infected with a pathogen. Choice C is incorrect because *contaminant* is a more general term that can refer both to microorganisms—which fall into the category of biological contaminants—and other types of contaminants, including toxins, chemical contaminants, and physical contaminants. Choice D is incorrect because a diagnosis is the identification of a disease. While the name of an individual diagnosis may be the same as, or based on, the name of the pathogen that caused it (for example, a diagnosis of salmonellosis or hepatitis A), the term *diagnoses* does not refer to disease-causing microorganisms in general.

**35. D:** Receipt of a delivery should include a visual review of the truck to look for any signs of contamination, such as bug infestation or rodent droppings. Examining the outside of the truck, Choice C, is not necessary, nor is a judgement about the visual appearance of the delivery driver, Choice B. The purchase order, Choice A, should have been reviewed upon placement of the order, rather than when the delivery has arrived.

**36. D:** Choice D states that raw foods should be stored away from ready-to-eat foods to prevent cross-contamination. Choice A is incorrect as storing food in the temperature danger zone should generally be avoided as it encourages bacterial growth. Choice B is incorrect as storing older foods behind newer foods can allow older foods to go bad before being used. Choice C is incorrect; while food should be kept out of the temperature danger zone, there are other things to keep in mind when storing food (such as avoiding cross-contamination).

**37. A:** Choice A is correct; when food is being marinated, it should be refrigerated. Choice B is incorrect because this could lead to food being stored within the temperature danger zone. Choice C is incorrect;

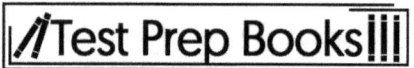

Answer Explanations #1

while marinated food can be frozen, it is not the only way to hold marinated food. Choice D is incorrect because while boiling a marinade may kill germs within it, it does not make the temperature that it's held at irrelevant.

**38. C:** The five foodborne illness risk factors are food from unsafe sources, inadequate cooking, improper holding times and temperatures, contaminated equipment, and poor personal hygiene. Choice A is incorrect because, although employee training does impact each of the five foodborne illness risk factors, it is not specifically identified by the CDC as one of those five factors. Choice B is incorrect because, although improper hand washing does contribute significantly to foodborne illnesses, in reference to the five foodborne illness risk factors, hand washing falls into the broader category of poor personal hygiene. Choice D is incorrect because, although fecal contamination does contribute significantly to foodborne illnesses and is strongly related to poor personal hygiene, food from unsafe sources, and contaminated equipment, it is not itself one of the CDC's five foodborne illness risk factors.

**39. A:** Fresh meat and poultry should be checked by placing a thermometer directly into the thickest part of the meat. The thinnest part of the meat, Choice B, would not give an accurate reading for larger sections or pieces of meat. Choice C, placing a thermometer between two packages of meat, or by folding the package around the thermometer, Choice D, is used for meat that is vacuum-sealed.

**40. B:** Cold food items, such as meats, should be at least 41 °F or cooler. Choices A, C, and D are made-up answers.

**41. C:** Choice C is correct as fresh shellfish can be frozen for up to one year. Choices A and B are incorrect as fresh shellfish can be frozen longer than both six months and nine months. Choice D is incorrect as eighteen months is too long for fresh shellfish to be frozen.

**42. B:** The nine major food allergens are milk, eggs, fish, crustacean shellfish, tree nuts, wheat, peanuts, soybeans, and sesame. Choice A is incorrect and is a list of foods that have a higher likelihood of causing foodborne illness. Choice C is incorrect, and only three of the items—dairy, nuts, and seeds—are associated with the nine major food allergens. Choice D is incorrect because these are specific foods that fall into eight of the broader categories that make up the nine major food allergens.

**43. D:** Choice D is correct because the only choice provided that is not a TCS food is uncooked beans. The other choices are all TCS foods.

**44. A:** Insulation and other physical hazards can cause physical contamination. Choice B is incorrect because contamination with *Shigella* bacteria is considered biological contamination. Choice C is incorrect because contamination with mercury is considered chemical contamination. Choice D is incorrect because contamination with ciguatoxin is considered chemical contamination from a naturally occurring chemical.

**45. A:** Because the illness, toxoplasmosis, is caused by the pathogen itself—in this case the *Toxoplasma gondii* parasitic protozoan—it is classified as a foodborne infection. Choice B is incorrect because a physical hazard is an object that is present in food—such as bone fragments or staples. If classifying the *Toxoplasma gondii* parasite as a type of hazard, it would fall into the category of biological hazards rather than physical hazards. Choice C is incorrect because toxoplasmosis is common and is the second leading cause of foodborne illness-related deaths in the US. Choice D is incorrect because, although toxoplasmosis is more prevalent in some countries than in others, it is by no means isolated to developing countries, so this would not be the best classification for it.

Answer Explanations #1

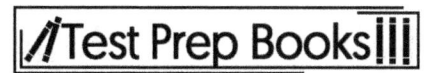

**46. A:** Choice *A* is correct as it is a sanitary personal hygiene practice to wash hands in warm soapy water for at least twenty seconds. Choice *B* is incorrect because jewelry on the hands should be avoided. Choice *C* is incorrect because hair should be contained by a hair restraint when preparing food. Choice *D* is incorrect because employees should keep personal food away from where food is being prepared for customers.

**47. B:** Even minuscule amounts of food allergens can affect allergic individuals, so food contact surfaces on equipment and utensils must be free of any previous contamination from food allergens. Choice *A* is incorrect because rinsing food is not recommended for removing food allergens. Choice *C* is incorrect because pasteurizing and cooking are not effective means of protection against allergic reactions. Choice *D* is incorrect because any contact of a food allergen with food that will be consumed by an allergic individual could cause a reaction. Food that has had any contact with a food allergen to which the customer is allergic should not be served to that customer.

**48. C:** Breathing difficulty—along with itching, swelling, dizziness, and gastrointestinal symptoms—is a common symptom of a food allergy reaction. Choice *A*, jaundice, is yellowing of the eyes and skin, which is not commonly associated with food allergies but rather with liver dysfunction related to hepatitis infections. Choice *B*, tingling around the mouth, is not commonly associated with food allergies but rather with poisoning due to a fish toxin. Choice *D*, weight loss, is not commonly associated with food allergies but can be a result of other persistent foodborne illnesses, such as cyclosporiasis.

**49. C:** Egg dishes that will be hot-held for service must be cooked to a minimum internal temperature of 155 °F for 17 seconds. The other choices are incorrect because the temperatures that they state are either too low or too high.

**50. A:** Pests can enter a building through the tiniest of openings, including cracks, gaps, and holes in walls, floors, ceilings, and window and door surrounds. These should all be checked for and repaired regularly. While there may be evidence of pests in dry storage, Choice *B*, this is not usually an access point to the building, nor are the areas beneath equipment, counters, and tables, Choice *C*, even though there may be evidence of infestation in these places. Similarly, Choice *D* can provide evidence of pests, but these are not entry points.

**51. C:** Michelle did everything right with this delivery, except that the shellfish did not cool to at least 41 degrees within four hours. The fish was delivered at the right temperature, Choice *A*, and was put into the refrigerator quickly, Choice *B*. The time on the truck, Choice *D*, does not matter as much as the delivery temperature and getting the seafood cooled further within four hours.

**52. B:** A sign that food has thawed and refrozen is ice crystals on the packaging. Choice *A* is incorrect because thawing and refreezing will not necessarily break the packaging. Choice *C* is incorrect as the packaging being bloated can signify that the food is no longer good, not that the food has thawed and refrozen. Choice *D* is incorrect as food being discolored does not indicate if it has thawed and refrozen.

**53. B:** Bacteria like *Clostridium perfringens*, *Clostridium botulinum*, and *Staphylococcus aureus* cause illness by creating toxins. Choice *A* is incorrect because bacteria can grow outside of the danger zone but do so more slowly. Choice *C* is incorrect because some bacteria can survive cooking; for example, they sometimes form heat-resistant spores. Choice *D* is incorrect because bacterial infections usually have an incubation period between the time of infection and the appearance of symptoms, usually between 12 and 72 hours.

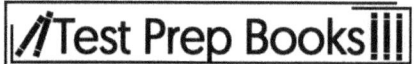

Answer Explanations #1

**54. C:** When cooling hot food, the temperature of the food must decrease from 135 °F to 70 °F within 2 hours and from 135 °F to 41 °F within 6 hours, allowing for a maximum of 6 hours in the danger zone. Choices A and B are acceptable amounts of time for the lasagna to remain in the danger zone temperature range, but they are not the maximum. Choice D is incorrect because 8 hours is too long for the lasagna to remain in the danger zone and still be safe to consume.

**55. A:** Choice A is correct because it states the correct process for preparing produce. Produce should be inspected, and rotten or damaged produce should be removed before being rinsed and cut. This includes produce that has a skin or rind that is not eaten. Choice B is incorrect as it states that produce that has skin that is not eaten does not need to be rinsed. Choice C is incorrect because it states that produce is rinsed before being checked for any rotten produce or damaged pieces. Choice D is incorrect as it states that produce should be washed with soap, which is not necessary.

**56. D:** Norovirus is the primary cause of foodborne illness in the US. Choices A, B, and C are incorrect because *E. coli*, *Salmonella*, and mold are less common causes of foodborne illness in the US.

**57. C:** Hepatitis A is a virus. Choices A, B, and D are incorrect because disease-causing bacteria, parasites, and fungi are pathogens that are classified separately from viruses.

**58. D:** Choice D is correct because the minimum internal temperature that raw poultry and fowl must be cooked to is 165 °F. The other choices are incorrect because the temperatures that they state are too low.

**59. C:** The GAP guidelines can be found in the *Guidance for Industry: Guide to Minimize Microbial Food Safety Hazards for Fresh Fruits and Vegetables* publication. Choices A, B, and D are other federal government publications.

**60. B:** Too much copper in food is considered a chemical hazard due to a toxic element, so when it causes illness, the illness is categorized as a foodborne intoxication. Choice A is incorrect because foodborne infections are illnesses caused directly by pathogens. Choice C is incorrect because copper that is leached into food in microscopic amounts is not considered a physical hazard. Fragments of metal, such as bits from a metal can, or other metal objects like jewelry that could cause physical injuries—including cuts, infections, or broken teeth—would be considered physical hazards, as would other nonfood objects like plastic, artificial fingernails, bone, or glass. Choice D is incorrect because Scromboid poisoning is a distinct foodborne intoxication that is caused by toxic levels of histamine in fish.

**61. B:** Choice B states 145 °F as the correct minimum internal temperature at which a pork roast must be cooked. It must reach this temperature for at least four minutes. Choice A is incorrect because the temperature is too low. Choices C and D are incorrect as the temperatures given are higher than the minimum.

**62. A:** A purchase order or receipt is necessary to ensure that the correct amount of the correct products is included in the delivery. In addition, a thermometer is used to ensure that the meats are delivered at the appropriate temperature. A scale, Choice B, is usually used for weighing produce, and a tape measure, Choices C and D, is not generally needed for food deliveries.

**63. C:** Because this is a new supplier, Manuel should not permit a key drop delivery. Key drop deliveries are reserved for well-respected, trusted suppliers. It is not always required for management or staff to

Answer Explanations #1

be onsite to receive a delivery, Choices *A* and *B*, if the supplier has been sufficiently vetted. Shipments should never be left unattended outside the restaurant, Choice *D*.

**64. D:** Choice *D* is correct as lamb chops can be refrigerated for three to five days. While the other choices contain lengths of time that lamb chops can be stored within the fridge, they are not the maximum.

**65. B:** Choice *B* is correct as hot-held food should be held at 135 °F and above. The other choices, while above 135 °F, are not fully accurate since the minimum temperature hot-held food can be held at is 135 °F. The other choices' minimum temperatures are all greater than 135 °F.

**66. C:** Training employees on proper hand washing and its importance for preventing foodborne illnesses is one way to address one of the five most common foodborne illness risk factors—poor personal hygiene. Choice *A* would be an ineffective way to check for toxin or pathogen contamination because the vast majority of toxins and pathogens are microscopic—they are not visible without a microscope. Choice *B* would not address any of the five foodborne illness risk factors since spreading pathogens from person to person among customers is not one of the foodborne illness risk factors. While Choice *D* does address a potential risk of physical contamination and is an advisable step, physical contamination through equipment such as thermometers is not considered one of the five most common foodborne illness risk factors.

**67. A:** Choice *A* states that egg yolks and whites being firm is one way, besides temperature, to know that eggs are fully cooked. Choice *B* is incorrect as not just the whites should be firm but also the yolks. Choice *C* is incorrect as not just the yolks must be firm but also the whites. Choice *D* is incorrect because the white and the yolks must be firm, not partially firm.

**68. A:** Old food should be replaced with an entirely new container of food, which should be covered as it is brought from the kitchen into the self-serve area. Choice *B* is incorrect since new food should not be mixed in with old food. Choice *C* is incorrect as the new container of food should be covered as it is brought from the kitchen to the self-serve area. Choice *D* is incorrect as the entire container should be replaced, not just the food that it contains.

**69. A:** The floor beneath all equipment should be cleaned and inspected every time the rest of the floor is cleaned. Choices *B, C,* and *D* are incorrect.

**70. B:** One in six people become sick with foodborne illnesses each year in the US. Choice *A* represents the number of hospitalizations each year in the US, and Choice *C* represents the number of deaths each year in the US. Choice *D* is incorrect because one in six is approximately 17 percent of the population, not 10 percent.

**71. D:** Choice *D* is correct because a high fever is often associated with the most common foodborne illnesses, along with diarrhea and vomiting. Choices *A, B,* and *C* are incorrect.

**72. B:** When a food service employee has an open wound, they may continue working in food preparation so long as the wound can be completely sealed and it's unlikely the wound or sealing will be torn open. Thus, Choice *B* is correct. Choice *A* is incorrect because a loose binding risks pathogens from the wound contaminating the food. Choice *C* is incorrect because even without visible bodily liquids (such as blood or pus), an open wound can still spread pathogens. Choice *D* is incorrect because a wound can contaminate food even if it is uninfected.

**73. B:** OSHA oversees the employees' right to work in a safe environment. Choice *B* is correct because OSHA mandates communication about hazardous chemicals by the manager to their employees, including training requirements. Choices *A* and *D* are incorrect because OSHA does not mandate the CPFM to share this information with employees (although doing so is best practice). Choice *C* is incorrect because OSHA mandates sharing a list of who is *allowed* to use pesticides, not a list of who is not permitted.

**74. D:** Choice *D* is correct because the inspection and documentation procedures recommended by an integrated pest management perspective do not reduce a facility's potential as a source of shelter for pests. For example, the facility can deny food and water sources, and inspections can reduce a pest's ability to access the building, but the building's walls, ceiling, pipes, and so on still provide a potential source of shelter.

**75. A:** Choice *A* is correct because mice, rats, and other rodents are capable of chewing through a plastic container. Choices *B* and *C* are incorrect because insects are not capable of doing so. Choice *D* is incorrect because while squirrels are a rodent capable of gnawing through plastic, squirrels typically avoid interior environments and are not a pest commonly encountered in the food service industry.

**76. B:** Choice *B* is correct because cockroaches tend to enter facilities through preexisting cracks in the wall, ceiling, or other parts of the building. These cracks are also a cockroach's preferred shelter. Choice *A* is incorrect because cleaning garbage bins prevents flies, not cockroaches. Choice *C* is incorrect because cockroaches are not particularly bothered by that temperature. Choice *D* is incorrect because proper food storage helps prevent all pests, not cockroaches in particular.

**77. C:** When a pesticidal spray is used, even when it's handled with caution there is a chance that the chemical will remain present on surfaces in the treated space. It's important to sanitize the room after using a spray to ensure that no chemicals contaminate food prepared there. Thus, Choice *C* is correct. Choice *A* is incorrect because, logically, this inspection should have been done prior to hiring the exterminator so that only a single service call is required. Choice *B* is incorrect because cleaning those rooms won't necessarily reveal potential infestations. Choice *D* is incorrect because the CPFM is not required to train employees to use a chemical that is not being used by any employees.

**78. C:** While it is true that the basics of the food safety code are largely determined by regulations set by the FDA (Choice *A*), USDA (Choice *B*), and CDC (Choice *D*), it is state and local regulatory authorities (Choice *C*) that parse out the specifics for each jurisdiction. It is important for food managers to familiarize themselves with the standards set by their local regulatory authority in addition to knowing the framework set by larger regulatory authorities.

**79. A:** Agents sent by health regulatory authorities (otherwise known as health inspectors) ensure that a food service establishment is complying with regulations set by the authority. As part of their inspection, they create a report of violations, recommend corrective measures, and sometimes penalize facilities that fail to comply. Choice *B* is incorrect because it is not their job to fix or maintain equipment. Choice *C* is incorrect because it is not their job to educate the staff. Choice *D* is incorrect because it is not their job to ensure customer satisfaction. Their role is to ensure compliance with the food safety code.

**80. B:** Acceptable reasons for sampling food product include Choices *A*, *C*, and *D*. Although it may be helpful for employees to be informed about the flavor of the food product, this is not listed in the food safety code as an acceptable reason for sampling.

# Practice Test #2

1. What is the industry-standard measurement used to determine the appropriate strength of sanitizer to water?
    a. mg/L
    b. ppth
    c. % m/m
    d. ppm

2. Cold-held food should be held at or below what temperature?
    a. 38 °F
    b. 40 °F
    c. 42 °F
    d. 44 °F

3. Alice is cleaning the food prep countertops in her restaurant. What does she need to do this job?
    a. Soap and water
    b. Sanitizing chemicals
    c. A wet rag
    d. A mop bucket

4. What are the key aspects of using chemical sanitizers?
    a. Concentration, temperature, pH, water hardness, and time
    b. Chemical, temperature, pH, water amount, and time
    c. Concentration, temperature, pH, water amount, and total application
    d. Concentration, time, preparation, water hardness, and total application

5. To allow for proper cleaning and maintenance, how high off the floor should floor-mounted equipment be?
    a. 5 centimeters
    b. 10 centimeters
    c. 15 centimeters
    d. 20 centimeters

6. What are the steps to properly cleaning a surface?
    a. Wipe surface with a towel, wash with soapy water, rinse, dry
    b. Remove debris and stuck-on materials, scrub with soapy water, rinse, dry
    c. Remove debris and food particles, scrub with soapy water, rinse
    d. Remove debris and stuck-on materials, scrub with soapy water, dry

7. What is the best way to ensure that equipment remains in good working order?
    a. Notifying management immediately of any issues
    b. Unplugging the equipment when it malfunctions
    c. Moving broken and/or nonworking equipment out of the food preparation areas
    d. Establishing a regular maintenance schedule

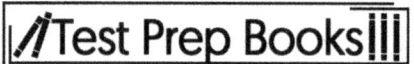

8. What is the proper order of cleansing and sanitizing when washing dishes by hand in a three-compartment sink?
    a. Rinse excess food off, cleanse, place within the sanitizing compartment, wipe dry
    b. Remove excess food, cleanse, rinse, place within the sanitizing compartment, air dry
    c. Place in the first compartment without removing food, cleanse, rinse, sanitize, air dry
    d. Rinse, sanitize, cleanse, air dry

9. What is the first step to cleaning and sanitizing equipment?
    a. Remove any removable part
    b. Scrape off any food scraps
    c. Unplug the equipment
    d. Air dry before reassembling

10. What happens when mixing a chemical sanitizer using water that is too cold?
    a. The chemical solution may separate and not mix appropriately.
    b. The chemicals will break down and become less effective.
    c. The solution will be too strong and could be hazardous.
    d. The solution will be too weak and therefore ineffective.

11. Where should handwashing stations be located?
    a. In dining rooms, restrooms, food prep areas, and food services areas, dishwashing areas
    b. In or near restrooms, food prep areas, and food service areas, dishwashing areas
    c. In dining rooms, behind the bar area, and in food prep and service areas, dishwashing areas
    d. In restrooms, bar areas, food prep areas, and service areas

12. Tabletop and countertop equipment should be mounted at least how high above the table or countertop?
    a. 5 inches
    b. 15 centimeters
    c. 6 inches
    d. 10 centimeters

13. Which federal regulatory agency sets forth the cGMPs?
    a. USDA
    b. CDFA
    c. NIH
    d. FDA

14. A shipment of food is received. The temperature of the cheese is 43 °F, the temperature of the uncooked rice is also 43 °F, and the raw frozen chicken is received with ice crystals. Which of these foods is safe to keep for consumption?
    a. The cheese
    b. The chicken
    c. The rice
    d. None of the food is safe to be kept.

15. What is one way to reduce the risk of physical contamination of food?
    a. Store food at or below 41 °F or at or above 135 °F.
    b. Avoid using sulfiting agents on raw fruits and vegetables.
    c. Pay attention to seafood advisories and reject potentially affected deliveries.
    d. Avoid wearing jewelry on the hands and arms when working with food.

16. At what temperature should hot foods be delivered?
    a. 130 °F
    b. 133 °F
    c. 135 °F
    d. 137 °F

17. Marcus has recently taken over as the food safety manager at a restaurant. He has discovered that the manufacturing guidelines for one type of product have not been reviewed or updated in quite some time. This could be a violation of which of the GMPs?
    a. Products
    b. Processes
    c. Procedures
    d. People

18. The five key aspects of GMPs are referred to as the five Ps. Which of the following is NOT one of the five Ps?
    a. Procurement
    b. People
    c. Premises
    d. Products

19. Which of the following is a TCS food?
    a. Uncooked pasta
    b. Whole, raw bell pepper
    c. Whole, raw melon
    d. Cooked onions

20. Based on current research related to food safety training, which action is most likely to improve a food employee's food safety behavior?
    a. Ensure technical training includes all applicable details related to the behavior.
    b. Schedule training in 2–3-hour blocks of time.
    c. Remind food employees that the same food safety practice expectations apply regardless of how busy the business may be at peak times.
    d. Offer rewards to employees who consistently implement food safety practices.

21. When a food employee must be restricted due to illness, this means that the employee:
    a. Is permitted to work but must not handle food or handle clean surfaces that will contact food
    b. Is not permitted to work
    c. Is only permitted to work while using single-use gloves appropriately
    d. Is permitted to work but must be carefully supervised to ensure that they are no longer symptomatic

22. A container of potato salad was prepared on March 2 by the manufacturer. Its expiration date is March 16. The restaurant opened the container on March 4. On which date should any leftover potato salad be discarded?
    a. March 16
    b. March 11
    c. March 9
    d. March 7

23. What is one important step for proper hand washing for food handlers?
    a. Wash hands in any sink large enough to allow for the hands and arms to be thoroughly washed.
    b. Remove jewelry, such as medical bracelets, while washing and replace only after completely drying the hands.
    c. Spend at least 20 seconds on the hand washing process.
    d. If washing with soap and water is not possible, use a hand sanitizer that meets FDA guidelines.

24. If a food thermometer shows both the Fahrenheit and Celsius scales, which best represents the accuracy required to ensure that temperature measurements are adequate?
    a. +/−1 °C
    b. +/−2 °C
    c. +/−1 °F
    d. +/−2 °F

25. Which of the actions below would be most helpful in case of a suspected foodborne illness outbreak?
    a. Have all staff members leave the premises prior to the arrival of investigators from the regulatory entity so that they are not in the way.
    b. Discard unneeded food items to prevent them from accidentally being used later after having been left in the danger zone during the investigation.
    c. Respond to investigators' questions with yes or no answers or as succinctly as possible, avoiding details that may detract from the matter at hand.
    d. Enlist the cooperation of food employees by explaining that open and honest communication with investigators will help protect customers.

26. Which of these reportable symptoms should be reported to the regulatory authority?
    a. Jaundice
    b. Lesion with pus that is not properly covered
    c. Vomiting
    d. Sore throat with fever

27. Food should be left out after cooking for no more than an hour when the air temperature exceeds which temperature?
    a. 70 °F
    b. 80 °F
    c. 90 °F
    d. 100 °F

28. Which of the following is true regarding the shelf life of condiments?
    a. Ketchup can remain unrefrigerated for up to six months.
    b. Condiments should be monitored as their shelf lives are different depending on different factors.
    c. Mayonnaise is an example of a condiment that is shelf stable.
    d. Condiments last longest when they've been opened and are refrigerated.

29. Occasionally there is a problem with the manufacturing process that results in items needing to be destroyed or returned to the manufacturer. What is the term for this?
    a. Rejection
    b. Recall
    c. Return
    d. Rescind

30. What is the process of receiving a shipment of food and storing it?
    a. Check all foods for safety and damage, throw out damaged or rotten produce, temperature check TCS and frozen foods, ensure frozen foods have not thawed and refrozen, separate unsafe foods, place raw foods away from ready-to-eat foods, place old foods within easy access
    b. Check all foods for safety and damage, throw out damaged or rotten produce, temperature check TCS and frozen foods, ensure frozen foods have not thawed and refrozen, throw out unsafe foods, place raw foods away from ready-to-eat foods, place old foods within easy access
    c. Check all foods for safety and damage, throw out damaged or rotten produce, temperature check TCS foods, place raw foods away from ready-to-eat foods, place old foods within easy access
    d. Check all foods for safety and damage, throw out damaged or rotten produce, temperature check TCS and frozen foods, ensure frozen foods have not thawed and refrozen, throw out unsafe foods, store food in the most convenient way

31. When considering food safety training best practices, which statement is true?
    a. Showing an employee how to do something, rather than simply explaining it to them, will undermine the employee and decrease their motivation.
    b. If initial food safety training is well designed, thorough, and accurate, no follow-up training should be needed.
    c. When noncompliance is observed, it is important to avoid embarrassing the employee by not addressing the matter directly but rather through group refresher training.
    d. Sharing the importance of food safety and the consequences of foodborne illnesses can help improve food safety practices by increasing employees' motivation.

32. What is the best way to handle food becoming contaminated in a self-serve area?
    a. Heat the food in order to kill any bacteria or viruses that could be within the food.
    b. Depending on what contaminated the food, there are different responses. If the food is contaminated through improper use of dishes or flatware, the food does not need to be replaced.
    c. Remove the contaminated container of food and replace it with an entirely new container of food, which is covered as it is brought out from the kitchen.
    d. Place new food atop the older, contaminated food in order to encourage the new food to be consumed first by customers.

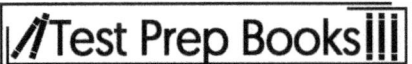

33. Which of these is one of the five foodborne illness risk factors and possible to mitigate by incorporating specific instructions into a written recipe?
    a. Inadequate cooking
    b. Food from unsafe sources
    c. Physical hazards
    d. Paralytic shellfish poisoning

34. What is the minimum internal temperature that ground turkey must be cooked to?
    a. 165 °F
    b. 160 °F
    c. 155 °F
    d. 150 °F

35. Which of the following foods should NOT be rinsed?
    a. Bean sprouts
    b. Romaine lettuce
    c. Canned beans
    d. Raw chicken

36. Which type of shelving is best for coolers and freezers?
    a. Wire
    b. Glass
    c. Plastic
    d. Metal

37. Anthony has noticed that raccoons seem to be getting into the outside garbage containers at his facility. What can he do to prevent this?
    a. Improve the lighting in that area.
    b. Take garbage outside less often.
    c. Improve the drainage to prevent liquids from pooling.
    d. Build an enclosure, such as a fence or wall, around the outside garbage areas.

38. Which of the following methods can be used to ensure that a thin chicken breast is cooked to a safe temperature?
    a. Check the inside of the chicken to ensure there is no pink color left.
    b. Insert a thermocouple thermometer sideways into the chicken breast.
    c. Check the temperature of the chicken with an infrared thermometer.
    d. Insert the tip of the stem of a bimetallic dial thermometer into the chicken

39. Allan is receiving a delivery and has set aside one item that must be rejected. He notified the driver and provided a description of the problem. He also made note of the incident in the store's delivery log. What did Allan forget to do?
    a. Take a picture of the rejected item
    b. Call and notify his manager of the rejected item
    c. File a formal complaint with the supplier
    d. Get a signed receipt from the driver

40. Once pasteurized egg liquids have been opened, how long can they be refrigerated?
   a. Three days
   b. Five days
   c. Eight days
   d. Ten days

41. Which of the following is true regarding handwashing practices for professionals in a restaurant setting?
   a. Employees should wash their hands for at least fifteen seconds in soapy water.
   b. If employees wash their hands well, it is okay for them to wear jewelry on their hands.
   c. Warm, soapy water should be used while employees wash their hands for at least twenty seconds.
   d. Only employees making the food should be careful about hand hygiene.

42. Many types of seafood have the potential to cause poisoning due to fish or shellfish toxins, but some carry such high risks that it is recommended they be avoided completely. To which of the following does this recommendation apply?
   a. Mackerel
   b. Oysters
   c. Whelks
   d. Pufferfish

43. What is the minimum internal temperature that a lamb steak must be cooked to for safe consumption?
   a. 160 °F
   b. 155 °F
   c. 150 °F
   d. 145 °F

44. Which of the following actions should be taken at least once per year?
   a. Ask food employees if they have experienced reportable symptoms or been diagnosed with a reportable diagnosis.
   b. Conduct food safety refresher training.
   c. Evaluate the types of thermometers used to measure safe cooking temperatures for each food item.
   d. Dispose of heavily used food contact vessels, such as cooking pans.

45. Bare hands should not be used when handling food that will not be further cooked to safe temperatures before being served UNLESS:
   a. The food handler has a latex allergy.
   b. The food handler is washing fruits and vegetables.
   c. The food is not considered a time/temperature control for safety (TCS) food.
   d. The food handler washes their hands immediately before handling the food.

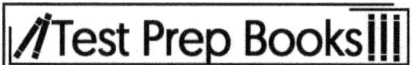

46. How should single-use gloves be used?
    a. Use gloves when hands may be contaminated to avoid contaminating food.
    b. Ensure the gloves do not tear by rolling them up before putting them on.
    c. When switching tasks frequently, use gloves if there will not be time for frequent hand washing.
    d. Food handlers with artificial fingernails or nail polish should use single-use gloves for all food contact.

47. How long can fresh eggs be stored in the refrigerator?
    a. Three to five weeks
    b. Two to four weeks
    c. One to two weeks
    d. Three to six weeks

48. How many reportable diagnoses are there?
    a. Four
    b. Five
    c. Six
    d. Seven

49. In an HACCP plan, if one identified critical control point is the step when prepared food is held in a warming oven before being sold, the minimum holding temperature of 135 °F during this step is referred to as:
    a. A critical limit
    b. A verification procedure
    c. The danger zone
    d. A control measure

50. How long can raw sausage be safely refrigerated?
    a. One to two days
    b. Two to four days
    c. Three to five days
    d. One week

51. What is true of the use of open condiments in a restaurant setting?
    a. Open condiments are not a contamination risk in terms of foodborne illnesses.
    b. All condiments need to be refrigerated during non-business hours.
    c. Most condiments have a longer shelf-life when left unrefrigerated.
    d. Condiments should be fully replaced when gone, not refilled into the older container.

52. What is the proper order for shelving items in refrigerators and coolers, from top to bottom?
    a. Produce and ready-to-eat foods, whole cuts of pork and beef, seafoods, ground meats and fish, poultry
    b. Seafoods, produce and ready-to-eat foods, whole cuts of pork and beef, poultry, ground meats and fish
    c. Produce and ready-to-eat foods, seafoods, whole cuts of pork and beef, ground meats and fish, poultry
    d. Seafoods, produce and ready-to-eat foods, poultry, whole cuts of pork and beef, ground meats and fish

53. How long can deli-sliced lunch meat be frozen?
   a. Nine months
   b. Three to six months
   c. Two to four months
   d. One to two months

54. Air curtains or fly fans are best used to prevent pests in what areas of the building?
   a. External doorways
   b. Swinging doors between the kitchen and dining room
   c. Attic and basement spaces
   d. Between the kitchen and storage areas

55. What are the proper temperatures and time frames for cooling food?
   a. Hot foods should reach 70 °F within two hours and 41 °F within the next four hours.
   b. Hot foods should reach 65 °F within two hours and 41 °F within four hours total.
   c. Hot foods should reach 70 °F within two hours and 41 °F within four hours total.
   d. Hot foods should reach 70 °F within two hours and 38 °F within four hours total.

56. How long can any cut of fully cooked ham be frozen?
   a. One to two months
   b. Three to four months
   c. Four to six months
   d. Nine to twelve months

57. Which of the following is true of sanitary practices that should be requested of customers in a self-serve area?
   a. Flatware can be grabbed by its head, so long as customers are encouraged to wash their hands.
   b. Plates can be reused by customers, so long as the self-serve utensils do not touch the plate.
   c. Signs should be posted that encourage customers to follow various sanitary practices.
   d. Sneeze guards should be used during cold and flu seasons and are not necessary during other times of the year.

58. What is the longest that ready-to-eat TCS foods can be safely stored?
   a. Three days
   b. Five days
   c. Seven days
   d. Ten days

59. What type of thermometer measures only surface temperatures?
   a. Thermocouple thermometer
   b. Thermistor thermometer
   c. Bimetallic stemmed (dial) thermometer
   d. Infrared thermometer

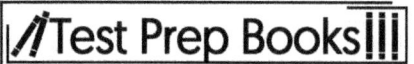

60. Which of the following is NOT true of employees working in a self-serve area?
    a. There should be employees who monitor the temperatures of the foods to ensure they stay out of the temperature danger zone.
    b. When replacing the food, employees should bring a full container of food to replace the old container.
    c. Employees should follow standard sanitary practices including having clean hands and a clean uniform.
    d. Employees must avoid working if they have had diarrhea or vomiting in the past thirty-six hours.

61. What are the proper steps for cleaning and sanitizing equipment?
    a. Shut off and unplug, keep on removable parts, wipe off anything that remains on the surface, wash with a cleanser, rinse, use sanitizing solution, air dry
    b. Shut off and unplug, clean and sanitize removable parts in either a three-compartment sink or dishwasher, wipe off anything that remains on the surface, wash with a cleanser, rinse, use sanitizing solution, wipe dry
    c. Shut off and unplug, clean and sanitize removable parts in either a three-compartment sink or dishwasher, wipe off anything that remains on the surface, wash with a cleanser, rinse, use sanitizing solution, air dry
    d. Shut off, clean and sanitize removable parts in either a three-compartment sink or dishwasher, wipe off anything that remains on the surface, wash with a cleanser, rinse, use sanitizing solution, air dry

62. Which symptoms should employees NOT have experienced for at least twenty-four hours before handling food?
    a. An infected cut on the hand
    b. Vomiting or diarrhea
    c. A sore throat and fever
    d. Jaundice

63. Which of the following is an appropriate way to handle glassware to keep its structural integrity?
    a. Glassware can be allowed to soak in the cleaning compartment of the sink.
    b. If a glass has ice in it, it can be dumped out and immediately placed in the dishwasher.
    c. Glassware can be stacked atop one another, so long as they are handled with care when transporting the stack.
    d. Avoid allowing glassware to come into contact with other glassware and items.

64. Under which of the following conditions should a food thermometer be calibrated?
    a. After the food handler has had an interruption, such as taking a phone call
    b. When the thermometer has been left in an oven during cooking
    c. After a time–temperature indicator has changed color
    d. When the thermometer has been used on frozen food and then on hot food

65. Checking shipment packaging for evidence of pests is part of which step in the pest control process?
    a. Deprivation of food and water
    b. Preventing access
    c. Treatment
    d. Inspection

66. In order to prevent pests from accessing food stored on shelves, how high off the floor should the shelves be lifted?
    a. 2 inches
    b. 4 inches
    c. 6 inches
    d. 8 inches

67. Allison is inspecting her building for pest entry points and has discovered two vents that are not covered. What should she use to cover these vents?
    a. Metal caps
    b. Boards
    c. Wire mesh screens
    d. Nothing; vents cannot be covered

68. Which of the following is NOT a service typically provided by a pest control company?
    a. Identify the source of the infestation.
    b. Seal cracks and other openings where pests are entering the building.
    c. Provide suggestions for prevention of future problems.
    d. Set traps and spray chemicals to help eliminate pests.

69. What is the minimum internal temperature that fish must be cooked to?
    a. 145 °F
    b. 150 °F
    c. 155 °F
    d. 160 °F

70. Hot-held food must stay at a minimum of 135 °F, however, temperatures above which degrees are preferable?
    a. 138 °F
    b. 141 °F
    c. 145 °F
    d. 155 °F

71. Which of the following situations is NOT required to be reported to a government authority?
    a. Employee slices their thumb with a knife
    b. Customer diagnosed with Hepatitis A
    c. Undiagnosed employee with diarrhea
    d. Customer illness due to shellfish allergy

72. An employee leaves work early due to vomiting during lunch. Which of the following must be documented by the CPFM?
    a. The date and time the employee left
    b. The employees sitting near the ill employee
    c. The employee's contact information
    d. The employee's health insurance information

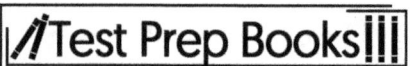

73. Which of the following is the MOST IMPORTANT reason a facility should avoid storing cleaning products in high-up places?
   a. Doing so disadvantages short employees.
   b. Products stored above eye level are more difficult to find in an emergency.
   c. Cleaning products at that height may drip chemicals onto surfaces below.
   d. Storing cleaning products should be stored in close proximity to potential messes.

74. A chemical contaminates a hamburger while it is being cooked due to the fuel used in the grill. What type of contaminant is this?
   a. Sanitizing contaminant
   b. Environmental contaminant
   c. Process contaminant
   d. Heat-induced contaminant

75. What is the right to routine inspections?
   a. An employee has the right to inspect their personnel and health records at their request.
   b. A food manager has the right to inspect an employee's personal belongings to ensure they have not brought contaminants that may compromise food safety onto the premises.
   c. A consumer has the right to inspect the kitchen to ensure their food is being prepared in a sanitary manner.
   d. A health regulatory authority has the right to inspect food service establishments to ensure compliance with the food safety code.

76. Which of the following is true concerning the process to correct violations found during a health inspection?
   a. Establishments must correct all violations immediately.
   b. Corrective actions may include employee re-training or implementing new food safety and/or sanitation procedures.
   c. Food managers are responsible for identifying violations and determining the necessary steps to correct them.
   d. It is unnecessary to document the corrections implemented as there will likely be a follow-up inspection.

77. Which of the following is an acceptable method for thawing food?
   a. Submerging it in cold water
   b. Leaving it on the counter
   c. Warming it in the microwave
   d. Putting it near a hot oven or grill

78. When it comes to foodborne illness, outbreaks due to one of the five major risk factors are typically due to:
   a. difficulty in predicting the behavior of pathogens.
   b. employees not properly and/or regularly implementing food safety procedures.
   c. food establishments procuring food from unapproved suppliers.
   d. improper training of employees.

79. How often should employees be re-trained in food safety measures?
   a. At least once every three months
   b. At least once every six months
   c. At least once a year
   d. At least once every three years

80. Thermal shock refers to:
   a. glass breakage due to its temperature changing too rapidly.
   b. the surge in bacterial growth when food is stored at improper temperatures.
   c. a type of sanitation procedure where pathogens are killed by exposure to very high temperatures.
   d. the physical response an employee can have when working in an excessively heated kitchen.

# Answer Explanations #2

**1. D:** Concentration is measured in parts per million (ppm), which should be checked using a test kit. Choice *A* is milligrams per liter. Choice *B* is parts per thousand, and Choice *C* is percentage composition by mass. These are all different ways of measuring concentration, but the industry standard is to use ppm.

**2. B:** Choice *B* states the correct temperature that cold-held food should be held below, 40 °F. Choice *A* is incorrect because 38 °F is too low. Choices *C* and *D* are incorrect as the temperatures 42 °F and 44 °F are too high and are in the temperature danger zone.

**3. B:** Food prep surfaces should be sanitized using specific chemicals designed to kill germs. Cleaning with soap and water, Choice *A*, is fine for walls and floors. Rags, Choice *C*, should not be used for cleaning, and a bucket used for mopping floors, Choice *D*, should never be used to clean food prep areas.

**4. A:** The five key aspects of using chemical sanitizers are concentration, temperature, pH, water hardness, and time. Choices *B*, *C*, and *D* are incorrect.

**5. C:** Floor-mounted equipment should be at least 15 centimeters (6 inches) off the floor. Choices *A*, *B*, and *D* are incorrect.

**6. B:** The proper way to clean a surface includes removing any stuck-on materials, scrubbing the surface thoroughly with soapy water, rinsing with clean water, and drying the surface with a clean cloth. Wiping the surface, Choice *A*, may not be sufficient to remove stuck-on materials, and the surface should be scrubbed. While some surfaces can be left to air dry, Choice *C*, drying the wet surface with a clean towel can help prevent spills and accidents. Choice *D* omits the step of rinsing the surface.

**7. D:** A regular maintenance schedule, both in-house and with a technician, can help avoid any problems with the equipment. While it's good practice to notify management of any issues, Choice *A*, along with unplugging malfunctioning equipment, Choice *B*, these are protocol and safety precautions after a problem is evident rather than preventative measures. Moving broken equipment, Choice *C*, is not usually a feasible option.

**8. B:** Choice *B* states the correct order regarding cleansing and sanitizing dishes in a three-compartment sink. First, excess food is removed from the dish before it is cleansed. The dish is then rinsed and sanitized. Lastly, it will air dry. Choice *A* states that the dishes are wiped dry. This is incorrect since they should air dry. Choice *C* is incorrect as it states that dishes are first placed in the sink without removing excess food, which is not true. Choice *D* states that dishes are sanitized before being cleansed, which is incorrect.

**9. C:** Equipment should always be unplugged before beginning any cleaning or sanitizing process. In addition, the manufacturer's instructions and recommendations should be carefully reviewed to ensure proper cleaning and sanitizing techniques and materials are used. Choices *A*, *B*, and *D* refer to other steps in the cleaning and sanitizing process.

**Answer Explanations #2**

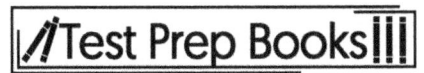

**10. A:** Using water that is too cold can result in a separated solution. Choice *B* is what happens when the water used is too hot, and Choices *C* and *D* are the effects of poor concentration, either too much or too little chemical to water.

**11. B:** Handwashing stations should be in or near restrooms, food prep areas, food service areas, and dishwashing areas. They are not necessary in or near dining rooms, Choices *A* and *C*, nor in bar areas, Choice *D*, though it is a good idea to have one in or near the bar as a best practice.

**12. D:** Table- and counter-mounted equipment should be at least 4 inches or 10 centimeters above the surface. Floor-mounted equipment should be 6 inches or 15 centimeters above the floor, Choices *B* and *C*.

**13. D:** cGMPs, or current Good Manufacturing Practices, are established by the Food and Drug Administration (FDA). While the USDA, Choice *A*, is a federal regulatory agency, it does not set forth the cGMPs. The CDFA, Choice *B*, is the California Department of Food and Agriculture, a regulatory agency in California (as opposed to a federal agency). The NIH, Choice *C*, is the National Institute of Health, a research and disease prevention agency that is not involved in food safety.

**14. C:** Choice *C* is correct because the only non-TCS food that is listed is uncooked rice. This means that the uncooked rice can be stored at temperatures above 40 °F without worry of the food being unsafe for consumption. Choice *A* is incorrect. Cheese is a TCS food that is being held in the temperature danger zone, meaning that it is not safe for consumption. Choice *B* is incorrect; the chicken seems to have been thawed and refrozen, which makes the food unsafe. Choice *D* is incorrect since the rice is safe to be kept.

**15. D:** Jewelry or parts of jewelry can accidentally fall off into food and create dangerous physical hazards for consumers through physical contamination. Choice *A* is incorrect because avoiding the danger zone, between 41 °F and 135 °F, will help control biological hazards by inhibiting the growth of certain pathogens. Choice *B* is incorrect because sulfiting agents are chemical preservatives that are considered chemical hazards when used improperly on raw fruits and vegetables in food establishments. Choice *C* is incorrect because observing fish advisories is a way to reduce the risks associated with chemical contamination of seafood at its source.

**16. D:** Hot foods should be delivered at a temperature of at least 137 °F or higher. Choices *A*, *B*, and *C* are all too cool to keep the foods safe.

**17. C:** Manufacturing procedures should be reviewed and updated routinely. Choice *A*, products, refers to both the raw ingredients and the final product, which should all meet quality standards. Choice *B*, processes, refers to the actual manufacturing, whereas the procedure is the guideline or standard for how the process is done. Choice *D*, people, refers to the training and specific responsibilities of the employees involved in the manufacturing process.

**18. A:** The five Ps are people, Choice *B*; premises, Choice *C*; products, Choice *D*; processes, and procedures. Procurement is not one of these, so Choice *A* is correct.

**19. D:** All cooked vegetables are TCS foods. Choice *A* is incorrect because pasta and other dry grains only become TCS foods when cooked. Choice *B* is incorrect because raw bell peppers are not a TCS food. Choice *C* is incorrect because melons only become a TCS food after being cut.

**20. D:** Offering rewards is a behavior-based training strategy, which research has shown to be more effective than knowledge-based training. Choice A is incorrect because, although it is necessary to include important details, including a lot of detail does not necessarily lead to a greater improvement in food safety behaviors. Choice B is incorrect because longer training sessions are not shown to be more effective than shorter training sessions. Choice C is incorrect because reminding employees of expectations does not aim to improve their motivation through addressing their attitudes and beliefs.

**21. A:** Food employees who have had certain reportable symptoms or reportable diagnoses may, under specific circumstances, be permitted to work; however, they will be restricted from food handling duties. Choice B is incorrect because the correct term for not permitting an employee to work is to *exclude*, not *restrict*. Choices C and D do not represent measures that would fulfill the requirements of restricting an employee due to illness.

**22. B:** Products should be discarded within seven days of opening, which would be March 11 in this example. This is true regardless of the expiration date from the manufacturer, Choice A. Choices C and D are made-up answers.

**23. C:** The hand washing process, from wetting the hands and arms to drying them, should take at least 20 seconds, and at least 10–15 seconds should be spent vigorously rubbing the hands and arms with soapy water. Choice A is incorrect because only dedicated hand washing sinks should be used to wash hands. Choice B is incorrect because no jewelry, other than a plain ring, should be worn when working with food. Choice D is incorrect because hand sanitizers cannot be used as a substitute for hand washing and should only be used as an optional step after washing hands.

**24. A:** Food thermometers that display a Celsius scale should be accurate to +/−1 °C. Choice B is incorrect because +/−2 °C is a less stringent accuracy requirement and may lead to food temperature measurements that falsely indicate a food is at a safe temperature. Choice C is incorrect because, although 1 °F is a smaller unit than 1 °C, and this standard would require more accuracy than +/−1 °C, this choice does not best represent the accuracy requirement. Choice D is incorrect because +/−2 °F is less accurate than +/−1 °C and is only an acceptable standard when a thermometer does not have a Celsius scale.

**25. D:** Encouraging food employees' cooperation in the investigation of a potential foodborne illness outbreak is helpful for the investigation. Choice A may not be helpful since investigators may need information from staff members to aid in the investigation. Choice B is incorrect because no food should be thrown away, as it may be needed to help determine the cause of the outbreak. Choice C is incorrect because investigators will need open communication and detailed accounts to help determine the cause of the outbreak.

**26. A:** When a food employee is symptomatic with jaundice—yellow eyes or skin—the regulatory authority must be notified and must provide approval before the employee returns to work. Choice B is incorrect because lesions with pus that are not properly covered are a reportable symptom that results in restricted duties, but reporting them to the regulatory authority is not necessary. Choice C, vomiting, along with diarrhea, is a reportable symptom that warrants exclusion from work but does not need to be reported to the regulatory authority. Choice D, sore throat with fever, is a reportable symptom that warrants exclusion or restriction, depending on whether the facility primarily serves a highly susceptible population (HSP), but reporting it to the regulatory authority is not necessary.

**27. C:** Once the air temperature in a room reaches or exceeds 90 °F, food that is cooling must be stored in a refrigerator within an hour. Otherwise, the food may remain in the temperature danger zone for longer than necessary.

**28. B:** Condiments should be monitored as their shelf lives are different depending on different factors such as whether they're opened, refrigerated, etc. Choice A is incorrect because ketchup can remain unrefrigerated for one year if unopened or for one month if opened. Choice C is incorrect because mayonnaise is not shelf-stable and should not be out of refrigeration for more than two hours. Choice D is incorrect because condiments' shelf lives are generally longer when they are unopened.

**29. B:** A product recall occurs when a problem occurred during manufacturing that was not discovered until after the product had been shipped to customers. Choices A, C, and D are made-up answers.

**30. B:** Choice B is correct as it states the correct process for receiving and storing a shipment of food. Food should first be checked to ensure it's safe for consumption. Damaged or rotten produce, TCS foods within the temperature danger zone, and frozen foods that have thawed should be thrown out. Raw foods should be placed away from ready-to-eat foods, and older foods should be placed where there is easy access to them to ensure they are used before they are unsafe. Choice A is incorrect because unsafe foods should be thrown out, not placed in a special separate area. Choice C is incorrect; foods that have thawed and refrozen are potentially unsafe (as well as TCS foods that are within the temperature danger zone), regardless of what the specific temperature is. Because they are unsafe, these foods should be thrown out. Choice D is incorrect because food should be stored carefully to prevent cross-contamination or older foods from going bad.

**31. D:** Sharing why food safety is important helps improve motivation by changing food employees' attitudes and beliefs, which is part of the evidence-based practice of behavior-based training. Choice A is incorrect because showing food employees how to do something incorporates a visual element into training and can help them build confidence in their ability to practice the behavior. Choice B is incorrect because refresher training is recommended at least once per year regardless of the quality of the initial training. Choice C is incorrect because specific feedback and correcting noncompliance are important elements of ongoing training on food safety practices.

**32. C:** Choice C is correct as contaminated food should be removed entirely and replaced with a new container. Choice A is incorrect because contaminated food should be removed. Some things that can contaminate food cannot be killed through heat. Choice B is incorrect because contaminated food is contaminated, regardless of the source of that contamination, and therefore should be replaced. Choice D is incorrect since older, contaminated food should be removed so it is not served.

**33. A:** Incorporating specific instructions for the cooking time and temperature into a written recipe will help prevent inadequate cooking. Although food from unsafe sources, Choice B, is a foodborne illness risk factor, it is one that must be addressed at the time of receiving food by ensuring food is only received from approved sources and is therefore outside the scope of a recipe card. Choices C and D are not among the five most common foodborne risk factors, and additionally, Choice D—paralytic shellfish poisoning—is due to toxins that cannot be deactivated by cooking.

**34. A:** Choice A is correct as it states the correct temperature that any cut of poultry or fowl should be cooked to (165 °F). The other choices are incorrect as the temperatures they state are all lower than 165 °F, which would make the ground turkey unsafe to eat.

Answer Explanations #2

**35. D:** Choice D states a food (raw chicken) that should not be rinsed due to contamination risks. The other choices—bean sprouts, romaine lettuce, and canned beans—are all able to be rinsed and are safe to rinse.

**36. A:** Wire shelving is best for coolers and freezers because it allows for proper airflow, which ensures the products maintain a suitable temperature. While glass and metal, Choices B and D, can help to prevent contamination from any leaks or spills, they also restrict the airflow, which impacts the equipment's ability to properly maintain temperatures. Plastics, Choice C, are not suitable as they are porous and can harbor bacteria as well as prevent proper airflow.

**37. D:** Outdoor garbage containers should be enclosed to prevent pests. Improved lighting can help with safety concerns, Choice A, and outside areas should have suitable drainage, Choice B, but these will not keep out pests like raccoons. Garbage should never be allowed to collect inside, Choice B, and should be taken outside as often as necessary.

**38. B:** Thermocouple thermometers can be used to measure the temperature of a thin food unlike bimetallic thermometers. Choice A is incorrect because visual indicators like color are not a reliable indicator of safety. Choice C is incorrect because infrared thermometers are only able to measure surface temperatures, and internal temperatures must be measured to ensure that food is safely cooked. Choice D is incorrect because the sensor of a bimetallic stemmed (dial) thermometer is usually 2–3 inches long, from the tip of the stem to the dimple, and this entire area must be inserted into the chicken to accurately measure the temperature, not just the tip.

**39. D:** The delivery driver should provide a signed receipt of adjustment or credit when an item from a delivery is rejected. Choices A, B, and C are not standard procedure for handling a rejection, although different facilities may have different requirements. Managers and staff should always have a clear policy for the procedures required by their particular facility.

**40. A:** Choice A is correct as pasteurized egg liquids can be refrigerated for three days after they've been opened. The other choices state lengths of time that are longer than the three days that they can be safely stored.

**41. C:** Employees should wash their hands in warm soapy water for at least twenty seconds. Choice A is incorrect because the minimum time for hand washing is twenty seconds, not fifteen seconds. Choice B is incorrect because jewelry on the hands should generally be avoided, even with clean hands. Choice D is incorrect because all employees should be careful about hand hygiene, not just those making the food.

**42. D:** Pufferfish, also known as fugu or blowfish, carry a high risk of tetrodotoxin poisoning, which is life-threatening, and these fish should be avoided. Choice A is incorrect because, although mackerel is associated with Scromboid poisoning and ciguatoxins, it is not as high-risk. Choice B is incorrect because, although oysters are associated with some types of shellfish poisoning, they are not as high-risk. Choice C is incorrect because, although whelks are associated with neurotoxic shellfish poisoning, this is not usually life-threatening.

**43. D:** Choice D is correct because the minimum internal temperature that a lamb steak must be cooked to for safe consumption is 145 °F. The other choices all state a temperature that is above the minimum internal temperature that a lamb steak must be cooked to for safe consumption.

Answer Explanations #2

**44. B:** Food safety refresher training should be conducted at least once per year as a reminder of food safety practices. Choice A is incorrect, as food employees should report reportable symptoms and diagnoses as they occur. Choice C is incorrect because there is no prescribed recommendation for evaluation of which types of thermometers are used for each food item. This decision is made based on the suitability of the available thermometers to the food being measured and will likely remain the same unless the facility acquires new thermometers. Choice D is incorrect because, under normal circumstances, food contact vessels such as cooking pans can be used for longer than one year.

**45. B:** Food that will not be further cooked to safe temperatures is considered ready-to-eat (RTE) food and should not be handled with bare hands except when washing produce. Choice A is incorrect because a latex allergy does not exempt a food handler from wearing gloves. Nonlatex gloves should be provided, and utensils can also be used to prevent bare hand contact. Choice C is incorrect because gloves should be worn with RTE foods regardless of whether they are considered TCS foods. Choice D is incorrect because, unless the facility has the appropriate permit from a regulatory authority, bare hand contact is not acceptable even when hands have been washed.

**46. D:** Artificial fingernails and nail polish present a physical hazard when working with food and should be avoided or covered with single-use gloves when working with food. Choice A is incorrect because gloves should not be put on when hands are contaminated. Hands should always be washed prior to putting on gloves. Choice B is incorrect because gloves should never be rolled up while being put on. Choice C is incorrect because, while gloves should be changed when switching tasks, hand washing would be necessary anyway since it should be done before putting gloves on.

**47. A:** Choice A is correct as fresh eggs can be stored in the refrigerator for three to five weeks. Choices B and C are incorrect; while fresh eggs can be stored in the refrigerator for those given amounts of time as well (two to four weeks and one to two weeks respectively), they are less accurate than Choice A. Choice D is incorrect as fresh eggs can be stored safely in the fridge for up to five weeks, not up to six weeks.

**48. C:** There are six reportable diagnoses—the illnesses caused by norovirus, Hepatitis A, *Shigella*, Shiga toxin-producing *E. coli* (STEC), *Salmonella* Typhi (typhoid fever), and nontyphoidal *Salmonella*. Choices A, B, and D are incorrect because they do not represent the correct number of reportable diagnoses.

**49. A:** A critical limit in an HACCP plan is a numerical measurement, such as a temperature, used to determine whether safety standards are met at a critical control point. Choice B—a verification procedure—is a written description of how an HACCP plan's efficacy will be verified. Choice C—the danger zone—is the temperature range between 41 °F and 135 °F in which pathogens grow most rapidly, fostering contamination from pathogen overgrowth and toxin formation. Choice D—a control measure—is an action taken to eliminate or reduce the risk of a hazard at a critical control point.

**50. A:** Choice A states the correct length of time that raw sausage can be safely stored in the refrigerator. The other choices all state a length of time that is too long for raw sausage to be stored safely in the fridge.

**51. D:** Condiments should be fully replaced and not refilled into the old container. Choice A is incorrect as open condiments can be a contamination risk through their use and ability to go bad. Choice B is incorrect because not all condiments necessarily need to be refrigerated outside of business hours.

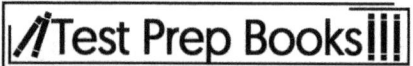

Answer Explanations #2

Choice C is incorrect; when not refrigerated, condiments' shelf lives are generally shorter than when refrigerated.

**52. C:** Produce and ready-to-eat foods, seafoods, whole cuts of pork and beef, ground meats and fish, and poultry should be stored in this order, from top to bottom. Foods should be stored so that any drips from meats or other possible contaminants do not get on fresh or other food items. In Choices A, B, and D, the fresh foods and seafoods could possibly be contaminated by the meats.

**53. D:** Choice D states the correct length of time that deli-sliced lunch meat can be frozen. The other choices all state a length of time that is too long for deli-sliced lunch meat to be frozen safely.

**54. A:** Air curtains and fly fans are used in external doorways to prevent bugs from entering through the open doors. Choices B, C, and D are incorrect.

**55. C:** Choice C states the correct time frames and temperatures regarding cooling food. Hot foods should reach 75 °F within two hours and 41 °F within four hours total. Choice A is incorrect as the food should reach 41 °F within four hours total, not four hours following the first two hours. Choice B is incorrect because hot foods should reach 70 °F within the first two hours, not 65 °F. Choice D is incorrect because hot foods should reach 41 °F within four hours, not 38 °F.

**56. A:** Choice A is correct as any cut of fully cooked ham can be frozen for one to two months. The other choices all state lengths of time that are longer than the length of time that fully cooked ham can be frozen.

**57. C:** Choice C states that signs should be posted to encourage customers to follow sanitary practices, which is correct. Choice A is incorrect since flatware should be grabbed by the handle. Choice B is incorrect because plates should not be reused in a self-serve area. Choice D is also incorrect; sneeze guards do not have a specific timeframe that they should be used within; rather they should be used generally.

**58. C:** Ready-to-eat TCS foods cannot be stored for longer than seven days. Choices A, B, and D are incorrect.

**59. D:** Infrared thermometers measure the surface temperatures of food and other equipment. Choices A, B, and C are types of thermometers with probes or stems that should be inserted into the food or liquid in order to register the temperature.

**60. D:** Employees must avoid working with food if they have had diarrhea or vomiting within the past twenty-four hours, not thirty-six hours. Choice A is incorrect because it is true that there should be employees who monitor the temperatures of foods to ensure they stay out of the temperature danger zone. Choice B is incorrect because it is true that when food is replaced, the entire container should be replaced. Choice C is incorrect because it is true that employees should follow standard sanitary practices including having clean hands and a clean uniform.

**61. C:** Choice C states the correct process to clean and sanitize equipment. Once the equipment is shut off and unplugged, the removable parts can be removed and washed separately. The equipment should be wiped clean of anything remaining on the surface before it is cleansed and rinsed. Then, the sanitizing solution should be used, and the equipment and its parts should be allowed to air dry. Choice A is incorrect as it states that removable parts should be washed along with the rest of the equipment.

Choice *B* is incorrect as it states that the equipment and its parts should be wiped dry after being sanitized. Choice *D* is incorrect as it only states that the equipment should be shut off, not that it should be unplugged.

**62. B:** Choice *B* is correct since it states that employees should not have had vomiting or diarrhea for twenty-four hours in order to handle food. The other choices are incorrect; while they are important symptoms to track in order to prevent illness from being passed through food, they each have their own protocol. It is not stated that they should not have occurred for twenty-four hours before handling food.

**63. D:** Choice *D* states that glassware should not be allowed to come into contact with other glassware or items, which is correct. This hurts the structural integrity of the glass and increases the risk of it breaking. Choice *A* is incorrect; glassware soaking in the sink can lead to glassware coming into contact with one another or other dishes. Choice *B* is incorrect because dumping the ice out of the glass and washing it in a dishwasher can cause thermal shock due to the temperature of the glass changing too quickly. Choice *C* is also incorrect, as glassware should not be stacked atop one another because this can lead to glassware being dropped and broken.

**64. D:** Food thermometers should be calibrated after extreme changes in temperature. Choices *A* and *B* are incorrect because these circumstances—an interruption in food handling tasks and being left in food while cooking—do not automatically necessitate calibrating the thermometer. Choice *C* is incorrect because time–temperature indicators are a type of temperature measuring device that cannot be calibrated.

**65. B:** Inspecting shipment packing for evidence of chewing or tearing, as well as inspecting for egg cases, droppings, and body parts, is part of the prevention step of pest control. Choices *A* and *C* are the second and third steps in the process. Choice *D*, while important, is not one of the specific steps in pest control.

**66. C:** Shelves should be raised at least 6 inches off the floor to prevent pests from accessing the stored items. Choices *A, B,* and *D* are not the correct distance.

**67. C:** Vents should be covered with wire mesh screens to keep bugs out while still allowing for suitable airflow and ventilation. Covering vents with solid materials such as metal caps or boards, Choices *A* and *B*, would restrict air flow. Vents can be covered if suitable material is used, so Choice *D* is incorrect.

**68. B:** Pest control companies do not generally perform works such as sealing cracks or other openings. They will, however, make suggestions as to how to prevent future pests, Choice *C*, including suggestions for sealing openings. They will also work to identify the source of the infestation, Choice *A*, and eliminate the pests, Choice *D*.

**69. A:** Choice *A* is correct as the minimum internal temperature that fish must be cooked to is 145 °F. The other choices are all higher than the minimum temperature that fish must be cooked to.

**70. B:** Temperatures of 141 °F or higher are preferable when keeping hot-held foods.

**71. C:** An employee with diarrhea is not permitted to work in food preparation, but without a doctor's diagnosis of a reportable illness, reporting this symptom is not mandatory. Thus, Choice *C* is correct. Choice *A* is incorrect because an on-the-job injury must be reported to OSHA. Choices *B* and *D* are incorrect because all customer reports of illness must be reported, regardless of cause.

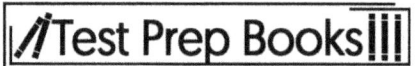

Answer Explanations #2

**72. A:** Choice A is correct because illness documentation must include the date it's recorded and the date symptoms began (in this case, they're one and the same). Choice B is incorrect because the CPFM is not obligated to document information about other persons. Choices C and D are incorrect because the documentation does not require additional personal information (some of which is protected under other labor laws).

**73. C:** Choice C is correct because any hazardous chemical that is placed or stored above other surfaces risks the lower surface becoming contaminated due to dripping nozzles, lids, etc. Choice A is incorrect because this is less important than avoiding foodborne illness. Choice B is incorrect because ease of access is less important than safe storage. Choice D is incorrect because storage near potential messes in the food service industry logically implies the cleaning product would be stored near food, which increases the risk of contamination.

**74. C:** Any contaminant that enters food while it is being cooked or prepared is considered a process contaminant by the FDA. Thus, Choice C is correct. Choices A and D are incorrect because these terms are not recognized as specific types of contaminants. Choice B is incorrect because environmental contaminants enter food from the ecosystem.

**75. D:** The right to routine inspections refers to a health regulatory authority's right to conduct routine inspections to ensure that a food service establishment is complying with the food safety code; therefore, Choice D is correct.

**76. B:** Choice B is correct because employee re-training and implementing new procedures are common corrective actions taken when an establishment is shown to be in violation of regulations set by health regulatory authorities. Choice A is incorrect because violations fall into two categories: critical and non-critical. Establishments must correct critical violations first. Choice C is incorrect because violations are identified by inspectors sent by health regulatory authorities, and corrective actions are generally prescribed by them as well. Choice D is incorrect because although it is likely that there will be a follow-up inspection, this is not necessarily the case. Additionally, whether or not there is a follow-up, it is important to collect documentation and evidence of corrective actions to submit to the regulatory authority.

**77. C:** Choice A is incorrect because cold water must be flowing for this to be a safe thawing method; stagnant water is not acceptable. Choices B and D are incorrect because thawing food at temperatures at or above room temperature allows for bacterial growth. Acceptable methods for thawing include refrigeration, running cold water, and microwaving (Choice C).

**78. B:** The five major risk factors are generally due to human error, typically in the form of employees not properly or regularly implementing food safety procedures, especially during peak times, per choice B. Choice D, improper training, may be a factor in this issue; however, it is secondary.

**79. C:** It is best for employees to be re-trained at least once a year to keep the information fresh in their minds and reinforce the importance of food safety procedures.

**80. A:** Thermal shock refers to glass breakage when temperatures change too rapidly. This can be avoided by allowing glass to come to room temperature before cleaning it in hot water or a heated dishwasher, and before adding cold beverages and ice.

# Practice Test #3

1. Suzette is having new lighting installed in her restaurant. Where should she look to find out the lighting requirements for the kitchen and food prep areas?
    a. FDA
    b. USDA
    c. Local ordinances
    d. County building codes

2. Which of the following is true of the differences between the three safe ways to thaw frozen foods?
    a. The microwave is the safest way to thaw food that has been frozen.
    b. Food should be cooked immediately after being thawed in the microwave or cold water. If food is thawed in the fridge, it does not have to be cooked immediately after thawing.
    c. Thawing food in the refrigerator can potentially allow for more bacteria to grow in comparison to thawing food in the microwave or submerging it in a sink filled with cold water.
    d. Thawing food in the sink is the most time-consuming option.

3. Which of the following are part of a building's systems and utilities?
    a. Plumbing, lighting, ventilation, and waste disposal
    b. Floors, walls, ceilings, windows, and doors
    c. Coolers and freezers, counters, and storage shelving
    d. Ventilation, floors and walls, coolers and freezers, and waste disposal

4. How is the intensity of lighting measured?
    a. Lumens
    b. Luminous flux
    c. Ohms
    d. Lux

5. Which of the following is true of the use of a dishwasher in cleaning and sanitizing dishes?
    a. All dishes that are used in preparing food can go in the dishwashers used in professional establishments.
    b. High-temperature dishwashers are unable to be used for glassware.
    c. Both chemical and high-temperature dishwashers can clean and sanitize dishes.
    d. The dishwasher should be used for sanitizing dishes, while the three-compartment sink should be used for cleaning dishes.

6. Danielle has a large stack of dishes to wash after the dinner rush as her restaurant. Which items should be washed in the dishwasher, and which items should be washed by hand?
    a. Utensils, plates, and the slicer blades by hand; pots and frying pans in the dishwasher
    b. Utensils, plates, and the slicer blades in the dishwasher; pots and frying pans by hand
    c. Utensils, plates, and frying pans in the dishwasher; slicer blades and pots by hand
    d. Utensils and plates in the dishwasher; frying pans, pots, and slicer blades by hand

7. The dishwashing machine at The Rose Café does not seem to be getting the dishes clean. Albert has inspected the machine and discovered that the high temperature thermometer is showing the water temperature to be 160 degrees Fahrenheit. What should he do?
    a. Call the maintenance department; the temperature is too low.
    b. Call the maintenance department; the temperature is too high.
    c. Nothing; that temperature is within the allowable range.
    d. Even though the temperature is within the allowable range, he should call the maintenance department to see why the machine isn't working well.

8. Which of the following is NOT something to inspect when performing a daily check of the dishwashing machine?
    a. The spray nozzles are clean.
    b. Machine is free of food debris.
    c. There are no mineral deposits.
    d. The racks are stable and firmly attached.

9. What is a vacuum breaker?
    a. A reverse fan used to keep bugs and pets out
    b. A stove fan that draws air up and away from the food prep area
    c. A valve that prevents water from traveling back up a hose
    d. An electrical fuse that prevents malfunction in the ventilation system

10. What creates a cross connection with regards to water and plumbing?
    a. The space between the faucet and the edge of the sink
    b. A hose attached to the sink with the other end in a mop bucket
    c. The space between the bottom drain of the sink and the floor
    d. A sink where the faucet is also a handheld sprayer

11. What is backflow?
    a. When dirty water travels back up a hose to a clean water source
    b. When air and odors are drawn up from the food prep areas through the ventilation system
    c. When swinging kitchen doors allow odors to escape into the dining areas and other parts of the building
    d. When bugs and pests enter a building through the fly fans

12. Which building system prevents the build-up of heat, smoke, steam, and condensation?
    a. HVAC
    b. Ventilation
    c. Plumbing
    d. Electrical

13. Cold ready-to-eat TCS foods must maintain what temperature?
    a. 45 °F or lower
    b. 35 °F or lower
    c. 38 °F or lower
    d. 41 °F or lower

Practice Test #3

14. What is the proper process to safely thaw food in a sink?
    a. The food can be removed from the packaging and submerged in cold water in a sink other than the three-compartment sink. The water should be replaced every half hour or so to keep the water cold.
    b. The sealed food should be placed in a sink of cold water. This should not be done in the three-compartment sink. The water should be replaced every hour or so to keep the water cold.
    c. The food should be sealed and placed in a sink of cold water. This should not be done in the three-compartment sink. The water should be replaced every half hour or so to keep the water cold.
    d. The food should be sealed and submerged in cold water in whatever sink is available. The water should be replaced every half hour or so in order to keep the water cold.

15. Which of the following is true regarding a Hazard Analysis Critical Control Point (HACCP) plan?
    a. It is a comprehensive approach to preventing foodborne illnesses in a food establishment.
    b. It is required for all food establishments.
    c. It assists in achieving active managerial control of foodborne illness risk factors.
    d. It should include control measures to address any potential hazards identified at a food establishment.

16. Gloria has received a shipment that includes a few new items for which the restaurant does not yet have regular storage space. Gloria decides to put the items into several large, airtight totes that she labels with the items, delivery date and supplier information. She stacks them out of the way in the employee locker room until space can be made in the pantry. The next day, the health inspector arrives and writes up a violation for the items. What did Gloria do wrong?
    a. She did not include the expiration dates on the totes.
    b. She did not store the totes in a suitable, food-specific location.
    c. The totes created a fire hazard by being in the employee's locker room.
    d. Items stored in non-food designated areas can only be stored for twenty-four hours.

17. Raul is inspecting a food shipment and notices that some of the packages on a particular pallet are chewed or torn. He suspects there might be a pest infestation with that pallet. What should he do?
    a. Accept the other parts of the shipment and tell the driver he won't accept that pallet
    b. Call his manager
    c. Leave the pallet on the truck and call the pest control company
    d. Refuse the shipment

18. If a nursing home food employee attended an event on Thursday evening where they were served food implicated in a disease outbreak, under what circumstances would restriction be necessary for the food employee reporting to work on Monday morning with no unusual symptoms?
    a. The outbreak was due to norovirus.
    b. The outbreak was due to ciguatoxin.
    c. The outbreak was due to Hepatitis A.
    d. The outbreak was due to *Listeria monocytogenes*.

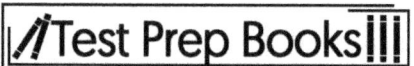

19. Which of the following best describes the concept of active managerial control?
    a. The food safety manager proactively sets up and monitors routine procedures for controlling foodborne illness risk factors.
    b. The food safety manager rotates among all food employee positions on a regular basis to identify and evaluate hazards associated with each role.
    c. The food safety manager responds to potential foodborne illness outbreaks by closing the facility, notifying the regulatory authority, and cooperating in all investigation efforts.
    d. The food safety manager uses appropriate temperature measuring devices, such as food and equipment thermometers, to ensure food is held at safe temperatures and sufficiently cooked.

20. Which of the following is NOT a concern when inspecting a delivery?
    a. Packages that are bloated or leaking
    b. Signs of dampness or water stains
    c. Discoloration or stickiness
    d. Fresh meats that have been wrapped in cellophane

21. How long can fresh ground poultry be safely stored in the freezer?
    a. One to two months
    b. Three to four months
    c. Five to seven months
    d. Six to nine months

22. Adriana is receiving a shipment that includes several cases of canned goods. One of the cases contains cans that appear to be dented, and a couple of the cans are missing their labels, though the delivery driver says all the cans in the case are the same product. What should Adriana do?
    a. Accept the delivery; dents are not a problem, and the contents of the cans is known.
    b. Reject the delivery due to the dents and missing labels.
    c. Accept the delivery with a certified statement from the driver regarding the products' safety.
    d. Reject the delivery due to the dents, even though the contents of the cans is known.

23. If a food establishment has a written process specifying that once per week, the general manager will review the food temperature log maintained by the kitchen manager to ensure the records are adequate and that appropriate corrective actions are taken, which HACCP principle is it applying?
    a. Establish verification procedures.
    b. Establish corrective actions.
    c. Establish monitoring procedures.
    d. Establish record-keeping procedures.

24. Travis is making a batch of coleslaw on October 12 that the restaurant will begin using immediately. The mayonnaise that he is using has an expiration date of October 16. What expiration date should be put on the label?
    a. No label is needed on freshly made items.
    b. No expiration date is needed because the food is being used immediately.
    c. October 16
    d. October 19

25. If an item from a delivery needs to be rejected, what should be done with the item immediately?
    a. It should be thrown away.
    b. It should be given back to the driver.
    c. It should be separated from the rest of the delivery.
    d. It should be put away with the rest of the stock but with a note not to use.

26. What type of shellfish poisoning is the most likely to occur and carries the most risk?
    a. Paralytic shellfish poisoning
    b. Neurotoxic shellfish poisoning
    c. Diarrhetic shellfish poisoning
    d. Amnesic shellfish poisoning

27. Which of these is the most appropriate way to cover a boil located on a food worker's finger?
    a. With an impermeable barrier, such as a cot
    b. With an impermeable barrier and a single-use glove
    c. With an impermeable barrier and a slash-resistant glove
    d. With a dry, tight-fitting bandage

28. A shipment of dairy goods has arrived at Denise's restaurant, and she has been tasked with receiving the delivery. She notices that the milk cartons have several different expiration dates. Today's date is February 27. Which of the following cartons should be rejected?
    a. Two cartons dated February 26
    b. Four cartons dated March 4
    c. One carton dated March 2
    d. One carton dated March 8

29. Sarah is storing items from a recent delivery. She is transferring some of the goods from their original packaging into larger storage containers that are labeled with the brand name of each product, the delivery receipt date, and the expiration date. What is missing from Sarah's labels?
    a. The common name of the product
    b. The name of the supplier
    c. The location of the manufacturer
    d. The phone number of the supplier

30. Which of the following foods can be held safely at room temperature?
    a. Pork roast
    b. Cooked beans
    c. Potatoes
    d. Ranch dressing

31. When using heat sanitization, the surface must reach what temperature and the surface must be soaked for how long for the sanitization to be effective?
    a. 171 °F for at least thirty seconds
    b. 165 °F for at least thirty seconds
    c. 180 °F for at least sixty seconds
    d. 176 °F for at least sixty seconds

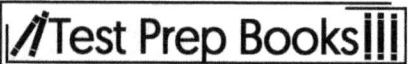

32. Which of the following situations risks cross-contamination of food?
    a. Using the same knife to cut poultry and then slice pork
    b. Rotating packaged meat with bare hands
    c. Thawing raw beef on the bottom shelf of a reach-in fridge
    d. Mixing lettuce, carrots, and celery for salad with gloved hands

33. The CDC recommends including which of the following core topics in a food service facility's policy manual?
    a. Food calorie information
    b. Utensil cleaning and maintenance
    c. Behavioral design
    d. Documentation procedures

34. Which of the following contaminants is least likely to be brought into a facility by an employee?
    a. Allergens
    b. Process contaminant
    c. Fecal matter
    d. *E. coli*

35. At what point in serving ready-to-eat (RTE) food is the risk of contamination greatest?
    a. When it's set out for the consumer to purchase
    b. When it's stored after preparation
    c. During the food preparation process
    d. During the food's delivery or transportation

36. A kitchen is cooking ground beef in preparation for batch cooking a casserole on tomorrow's menu. The employee cooks the beef in a microwave oven to an internal temperature of 150 °F, then begins to let it cool in shallow pans. The ground beef finished cooking at 4:00 PM. The ground beef must be cooled to which temperature or below at 6:00 PM?
    a. 100 °F
    b. 80 °F
    c. 41 °F
    d. 70 °F

37. What does the acronym MAP stand for?
    a. Modified atmosphere packaging
    b. Manufactured air package
    c. Manipulated atmosphere product
    d. Manufactured and packaged

38. Which of the following exemplifies a critical control point?
    a. The length of employee shifts
    b. The temperature to which food is heated
    c. The layout of the physical building
    d. The labeling of hazardous waste products

Practice Test #3

39. Which of the following increases the risk of foodborne illness?
   a. Storing fresh fruit at 35 °F
   b. Allowing prepared food to cool before refrigeration
   c. Serving ready-to-eat hot food for six hours
   d. Thawing frozen pork at 40 °F

40. How long does it take for illness-causing bacteria to double in food left in the danger zone?
   a. Four hours
   b. One hour
   c. 20 minutes
   d. 45 minutes

41. At 4:30 PM, the CPFM checks how long ingredients on their restaurant's salad tray have been sitting out, and their current temperature.

| Ingredient | Time Set Out | Current Temperature |
|---|---|---|
| Lettuce | 12:30 PM | 75 °F |
| Cucumber | 10:00 AM | 60 °F |
| Carrots | 2:00 PM | 45 °F |

The CPFM should remove and discard which ingredients?
   a. Lettuce
   b. Lettuce, cucumber
   c. Cucumber, carrots
   d. Lettuce, carrots, cucumber

42. An employee prepares soup stock for the evening meal on a sweltering summer day where the kitchen's temperature reaches 100 °F. How long may they allow the stock to cool before refrigerating it?
   a. Two hours
   b. Six hours
   c. Four hours
   d. One hour

43. A meal was cooked, and its internal temperature reached 165 °F. It sits on the counter for 30 minutes until the rest of the table's meals are ready. Its temperature has cooled to 80 °F when the CPFM checks it before serving. What is the correct course of action?
   a. Serve the meal
   b. Throw the meal away
   c. Make a new meal
   d. Refrigerate the meal

44. Which of the following devices is an appropriate way to keep ready-to-eat hot food at a safe temperature?
   a. Microwave oven
   b. Heat lamp
   c. Steam table
   d. Oven

45. Stirring reheated foods has which of the following safety benefits?
    a. Makes the food's texture consistent
    b. Ensures that the food's internal temperature is even
    c. Helps the food reach a safe temperature more quickly
    d. Allows the food to be set out for a longer time

46. What does the acronym "ppm" mean?
    a. Parts per meal
    b. Persons per menu
    c. Products per month
    d. Parts per million

47. Which of the following is a food safety benefit of paper wrappings on food served by a gas station?
    a. The paper prevents customers from touching the food, reducing the risk of contamination.
    b. The paper retains heat, allowing the gas station to leave it out longer.
    c. The paper provides space for a label with nutrition information.
    d. The paper prevents food crumbs from falling off the prepared meal and dirtying the facility.

48. Which of the following foodborne illness reporting standards is the most important?
    a. The FDA's standards
    b. The USDA's standards
    c. The local food code's standards
    d. The strictest standards

49. Which of the following is an appropriate way to provide food for self-service at a buffet?
    a. Open-air trays warmed by a steam table
    b. A table of warmed trays each covered with a sliding lid
    c. A full-size freezer with a scoop for serving ice cream
    d. Covered plastic basins containing salad ingredients

50. Which of the following pests does NOT require a source of standing water?
    a. Cockroaches
    b. Mice
    c. Rats
    d. Flies

51. A CPFM finds black droppings about the size of their pinky fingernail and damage to wooden pallets in their facility's storeroom. These are most likely signs of which of the following pests?
    a. Rats
    b. Owls
    c. Mice
    d. Bats

52. Keeping a clear space around the food service facility's walls is most likely to prevent which of the following pests?
    a. Cockroaches
    b. Sparrows
    c. Flies
    d. Mice

53. Which of the following pests is most attracted to an uncleaned garbage dumpster?
    a. Cockroaches
    b. Ants
    c. Flies
    d. Raccoons

54. Which of the following pests is most likely to enter a food service facility through a drainage or sewage pipe?
    a. Rats
    b. Mice
    c. Ants
    d. Flies

55. What does the acronym "FIFRA" stand for?
    a. Federal Insect, Fungus, and Rodent Alleviation
    b. Federal Insecticide, Fungicide, and Rodenticide Act
    c. Formal Insect and Fungus Reporting Act
    d. Former Insecticide Federal Relief Act

56. Documentation as required by health regulatory authorities refers to:
    a. The records, logs, and forms required to demonstrate compliance with food safety codes.
    b. The personnel and health records of employees.
    c. Records of employee misconduct.
    d. Permits and licenses held by the food service establishment.

57. Signage requirements—such as mandatory handwashing, non-smoking signs, and those outlining proper food handling procedures—are set by which of the following parties?
    a. The food manager
    b. The owner of the establishment
    c. The FDA and USDA
    d. The local health regulatory authority

58. The purpose of an HACCP plan is to:
    a. Protect food establishments from lawsuits.
    b. Protect employees from unsafe working conditions.
    c. Protect consumers from hazards caused by issues in the food production process.
    d. Protect employers from backlash after an outbreak of foodborne illness.

59. Which of the following is an example of active managerial control?
    a. Conducting background checks on potential employees
    b. Enforcing reporting policies for sick employees
    c. Making sure employees have consistent work schedules
    d. Having a system in place for arbitrating conflict between employees

60. What is the temperature range in which bacteria is most likely to thrive?
    a. 41°F to 135°F
    b. 41°F to 100°F
    c. 25°F to 135°F
    d. 25°F to 100°F

61. Which of the following are the most common viruses responsible for foodborne illnesses?
    a. Rhinoviruses and noroviruses
    b. Noroviruses and Hepatitis A
    c. E. coli and Hepatitis A
    d. Rhinoviruses and E. coli

62. Which foods are most likely to harbor viruses?
    a. Clams and oysters
    b. Poultry and eggs
    c. Beef and pork
    d. Wild game and fish

63. Which foods are most likely to harbor parasites?
    a. Clams and oysters
    b. Poultry and eggs
    c. Beef and pork
    d. Wild game and fish

64. Aflatoxin is a mycotoxin that can be found in crops such as nuts and grains, as well as milk. Too much exposure to aflatoxin can lead to death due to which of the following health complications?
    a. Diabetes and metabolic syndrome
    b. Cancer and liver failure
    c. Cardiovascular disease and blood clots
    d. Lung and esophageal issues

65. Which of the following is NOT one of the five leading causes of foodborne illnesses?
    a. Food from unsafe sources, such as unapproved facilities
    b. Not cooking food to the proper temperature
    c. Contaminated equipment
    d. Improper use of food additives

66. Contact with which of the following pathogens requires that an employee be removed from facilities serving a highly susceptible population for a period of at least thirty days?
   a. STEC or shigella
   b. Norovirus
   c. Typhoid fever
   d. Hepatitis A

67. Employees suffering from which of the following symptoms must report them to their supervisor?
   a. Vomiting
   b. Migraines
   c. Fainting
   d. Dizzy spells

68. Ready-to-eat TCS foods that will not be sold or consumed within twenty-four hours must be clearly marked with the date by which they should be consumed or sold. How many days after preparation is the expiration date for refrigerated ready-to-eat TCS foods?
   a. Three days
   b. Five days
   c. Seven days
   d. Nine days

69. Which of the following methods should NOT be used to speed the cooling of larger batches of food?
   a. Stirring the food in a container placed in an ice bath
   b. Using rapid cooling equipment
   c. Using a proofing cabinet
   d. Maximizing the exposed surface area of the food

70. Foodborne intoxications may be caused by which of the following?
   a. Pathogens like E. coli or Hepatitis A
   b. Naturally occurring toxins that accumulate in seafood
   c. Parasites such as toxoplasmosis
   d. Overgrowth of bacteria due to improper cooling and heating of prepared food

71. Corrective actions for addressing contamination occurrences include which of the following steps?
   a. Collecting data from the ill person concerning which foods they ate, the symptoms they are experiencing, and their contact information
   b. Writing up and/or firing the employees working at the time of the outbreak
   c. Contacting the local regulatory agency, such as the City Health Department
   d. Closing the facility to avoid additional exposure to the food causing the infection

72. Which of the following is NOT one of the nine major allergens?
   a. Gluten
   b. Soybeans
   c. Fish
   d. Eggs

73. Which of the following is NOT true when it comes to handling glassware?
   a. Glassware should be allowed time to warm after ice is removed and before being washed.
   b. Glassware should be allowed time to cool after being removed from the dishwasher before adding ice or cold beverages.
   c. Glassware should not be allowed to rest in the dishwater while being washed.
   d. Glassware should be stacked to enable an employee to carry multiples safely.

74. Which of the following is true concerning proper food storage methods used to prevent cross-contamination?
   a. Ready-to-eat food should be stored above raw food.
   b. Foods should be held at temperatures between 41°F and 135°F.
   c. Foods should be used last in, first out.
   d. Uncooked meat should be kept in a separate cooler from produce.

75. Which of the following is a major difference between cleaning and sanitizing?
   a. Cleaning removes bacteria, while sanitizing is required to remove viruses.
   b. Cleaning removes surface dirt, debris, and food particles, while sanitizing is required to remove bacteria.
   c. Cleaning requires specialized chemicals, while sanitizing can only be done with bleach.
   d. Chemicals used for cleaning can be stored at room temperature, while chemicals used for sanitizing have more specific storage requirements.

76. How often should food contact surfaces be cleaned and sanitized during periods of continuous use?
   a. Every two hours
   b. Every three hours
   c. Every four hours
   d. Every six hours

77. What is the general prescribed time range to allow a chemical sanitizer that contains chlorine to remain on a surface?
   a. At least seven seconds
   b. At least sixty seconds
   c. At least thirty seconds
   d. At least ten seconds

78. Which of the following is true concerning chemical sanitation?
   a. It only works on items that can be submerged in solution.
   b. Chemical sanitizers are closely regulated by the FDA.
   c. It is instantaneous.
   d. The most common sanitizers include chlorine compounds.

79. Which of the following is NOT a concern in the effective use of chemical sanitizers?
   a. The ratio of sanitizer to water
   b. The temperature of the solution
   c. The color of the solution
   d. Water hardness and pH

80. How often should machines that hold TCS foods such as ice cream and soda be cleaned?
    a. Daily
    b. Every other day
    c. Weekly
    d. Every other week

# Answer Explanations #3

**1. C:** Local ordinances regulate the lighting requirements for food prep locations. The FDA and USDA, Choices *A* and *B*, are regulatory agencies for food safety, but they do not regulate buildings and facilities. County building codes, Choice *D*, determine the structure of the building for its stability and safety, but they do not regulate lighting for the food industry.

**2. B:** Choice *B* states a correct difference between the three safe ways to thaw frozen foods. Food thawed in the fridge does not need to be immediately cooked, while if it's thawed in the microwave or sink it does need to be cooked immediately. Choice *A* is incorrect. Since the microwave can potentially partially cook the food, it must be immediately cooked for safety. Choice *C* is incorrect as thawing food in the fridge keeps the food out of the temperature danger zone, which means that bacteria cannot grow. Choice *D* is incorrect because thawing food in the fridge is the most time-consuming option, not the sink.

**3. A:** Plumbing, lighting, ventilation, and waste disposal are all part of a building's systems and utilities. Floors, walls, ceilings, windows, and doors, Choice *B*, are considered part of the facilities and equipment. Choice *C* is part of the equipment used in a facility, and Choice *D* contains a combination of all these things.

**4. D:** The intensity, or brightness, of lighting is measured in foot-candles, also called lux. Lumens, Choice *A*, are used to quantify the amount of visible light. Choice *B* refers to the measure of the total perceived light output, and Choice *C* is an electrical unit of measurement.

**5. C:** Choice *C* is correct; both chemical and high-temperature dishwashers can clean and sanitize dishes. Choice *A* is incorrect as not all dishes can go in dishwashers, regardless of the dishwasher being in the home or a professional establishment. Choice *B* is incorrect as high-temperature dishwashers can wash glassware. Choice *D* is incorrect as both the dishwasher and three-compartment sink can be used for cleaning and sanitizing dishes.

**6. B:** The dishwasher is good for washing utensils, plates, and other small items, such as the slicer blades. Large items like pots and frying pans should be washed by hand. Choices *A*, *C*, and *D* are incorrect.

**7. A:** The high temperature for most dishwashing machines should be between 165 and 180 °F. Albert needs to call maintenance. Choices *B*, *C*, and *D* are incorrect.

**8. D:** There is not usually a need to check the stability of the racks in the dishwasher unless they are clearly coming loose or have fallen. However, Choices *A*, *B*, and *C* should be inspected daily to ensure that the machine stays in good working order.

**9. C:** A vacuum breaker prevents backflow by shutting off the water supply line when the water is turned off.

**10. B:** A cross connection is a physical link between clean and dirty water. There should be space between the faucet and the sink edge and between the drain and the floor, Choices *A* and *C*, as these help prevent cross connections. There is no contamination risk in a faucet that doubles as a sprayer, as in Choice *D*.

**11. A:** Backflow occurs when dirty water travels back up a hose or other connection and contaminates a clean water source, such as a faucet. Choices B and C are made-up answers involving ventilation, and Choice D is a made-up answer because fly fans generally prevent bugs from being able to enter a building.

**12. B:** The building's ventilation system creates adequate airflow, which helps to prevent the build-up of heat, smoke, steam, and condensation. The HVAC system, Choice A, includes heating and air conditioning. Choice C is the water control system, and Choice D is the system that provides electricity to the building.

**13. D:** Cold ready-to-eat TCS foods must maintain a temperature of 41 °F or colder to prevent the growth of harmful bacteria. Choices A, B, and C are incorrect answers.

**14. C:** Choice C is correct as it states the proper process to safely thaw food in a sink. The food should be sealed and placed in a sink of cold water, but not in the three-compartment sink. To keep the water cold, it should be replaced every half hour or so. Choice A is incorrect because the food should not be removed from the packaging; it should be sealed. Choice B is incorrect because the water should be replaced every half hour or so, not every hour. Choice D is incorrect; the food should not be placed in any sink available since it should not be done in a three-compartment sink.

**15. C:** An HACCP plan is one element that a food establishment can incorporate as part of its approach to controlling foodborne illness risk factors. Choice A is incorrect because an HACCP plan is not comprehensive—it addresses particular hazards and must be used in addition to the facility's standard procedures, known as prerequisite programs. Choice B is incorrect because an HACCP plan is only required in certain facilities, not all. Choice D is incorrect because not all hazards identified at a food establishment must be addressed in an HACCP plan. Principe 1 of the HACCP system involves identifying any potential hazards and evaluating each one's likelihood of occurring and severity of the risk it could cause in order to determine which of the hazards will be addressed through control measures.

**16. B:** Food items should never be stored in non-food-specific areas, such as the locker room, no matter how well they are packaged and/or stored. Choices A, C, and D are made-up answers.

**17. D:** Any shipment that shows evidence of pests should be immediately refused. Accepting a partial shipment, Choice A, could be risky as there could be pests that are yet undiscovered. While the company policy may allow accepting a partial shipment, or may require that the manager be called, Choice B, the best practice is to refuse the entire shipment in the interest of caution. A pest control company generally will not inspect delivery trucks while they are on site, Choice C. It would, however, be a good idea for the delivery driver to contact his company and follow their guidelines for dealing with pests on their trucks.

**18. C:** Food employees who may have been exposed to the Hepatitis A virus through food involved in a confirmed disease outbreak within the past 30 days should be restricted from work in a facility that serves primarily highly susceptible populations (HSPs), such as a nursing home. Choice A is incorrect because potential exposure to norovirus necessitates restriction from facilities serving primarily HSPs only if the exposure occurred within the past 48 hours. Because Thursday evening to Monday morning is longer than 48 hours, the food employee does not need to be restricted when reporting for work on Monday. Choices B and D are incorrect because potential exposure to ciguatoxin or *Listeria monocytogenes* does not require restriction from work in a food establishment setting.

Answer Explanations #3

**19. A:** Active managerial control is a way to address foodborne illness risk factors through proactive, routine procedures. Choice B may be helpful for fulfilling principle 1 of the HACCP system—conducting a hazard analysis—but it does not describe the concept of active managerial control. Choice C is a true statement related to responding to a potential foodborne illness outbreak but does not describe the concept of active managerial control. Choice D describes a monitoring procedure that could be used as part of a food establishment's plan for active managerial control of foodborne illness risk factors, but it does not encompass the entire scope of the concept.

**20. D:** Fresh meats often arrive sealed in cellophane or other packaging. As long as the packaging is properly sealed, contains sufficient labeling (including expiration dates) and shows no signs of tampering, leaking, etc., it can be accepted. Choices A, B, and C can cause an item to be rejected.

**21. B:** Fresh ground poultry can be safely stored in the freezer for three to four months. Choice A is too little time and does not state how long fresh ground poultry can be stored in the freezer as accurately as Choice B. Choices C and D are incorrect as fresh ground poultry cannot be safely stored in the freezer for more than four months.

**22. B:** Products that have packaging that is dented and/or are missing labels should be rejected. A statement from the driver about the contents of the cans, Choices A, C, and D, is not sufficient.

**23. A:** In HACCP principle 6, verification procedures consist of a written description of the actions that will be taken to verify the HACCP plan's efficacy, including verifying that monitoring procedures—including maintaining a temperature log—are being performed properly. Choice B—establishing corrective actions, the fifth HACCP principle—would be applied through a written procedure for taking corrective action. In the example given, a protocol for how to respond to a food temperature measurement that does not meet the applicable critical limit, such as discarding or further heating the food, would be part of establishing corrective actions. Choice C—establishing monitoring procedures, the fourth HACCP principle—would be applied through a written procedure for how critical limits are to be monitored. In the example given, a procedure explaining that the kitchen manager is to check food temperatures on a regular basis would be part of establishing monitoring procedures. Choice D—establishing record-keeping procedures, the seventh HACCP principle—would be applied through a written procedure for how to record actions taken to fulfill prerequisite programs and HACCP plan procedures. It may include how monitoring measurements and observations, corrective actions, and verification actions are to be documented.

**24. C:** The product should be discarded by the earliest expiration date for any ingredient, or within seven days of preparation. In this case, the mayonnaise expires earlier than the seven days, which would be Choice D, so Choice C, October 16, is the date the leftover product should be discarded. Choices A and B are incorrect answers.

**25. C:** A rejected item from a delivery should be immediately separated from the rest of the delivery until it can be dealt with. The supplier should provide instructions as to whether the item should be thrown away, Choice A, or returned to the driver, Choice B. The item should never be placed with the usable supplies, Choice D.

**26. A:** Paralytic shellfish poisoning is the most common and most severe of the various types of shellfish poisoning. It can cause death in as little as 30 minutes. Choice B is incorrect because neurotoxic shellfish poisoning is less common that paralytic shellfish poisoning and is not usually life-threatening. Choice C is incorrect because diarrhetic shellfish poisoning is less common than paralytic shellfish poisoning and is not life-threatening. Choice D is incorrect because amnesic shellfish poisoning is rare and very rarely causes death.

**27. B:** When located on the hand or wrist, a lesion with pus, such as a boil, should be covered with an impermeable barrier and further covered by a single-use glove. Choice A is incorrect because, although an impermeable cot or other bandage should be used to cover the boil, the cot should further be covered by a single-use glove. Choice C is incorrect because the impermeable barrier (bandage, cot, etc.) should be covered by a single-use glove, which has an impermeable surface. Most slash-resistant gloves do not have an impermeable surface. Choice D is incorrect for a boil on the finger but would be appropriate for a boil located on a part of the body besides the exposed arms and hands. To be a sufficient cover for a lesion on the hand, the cover would also need to be impermeable and covered by a single-use glove.

**28. A:** Any item that is beyond its expiration date, even if that date is very recently passed, should be rejected. Choices B, C, and D can be accepted and should be stacked for use according to the earliest expiration date.

**29. A:** It is always a good practice to label items with the common name, such as "flour" or "sugar," rather than the brand name to avoid any confusion. Manufacturer and supplier information, Choices B, C, and D, are not necessary on the product labels, though the facility should have records of that information on file.

**30. C:** Choice C is correct as potatoes can be stored safely at room temperature. The other choices— pork roast, cooked beans, and ranch dressing—are all TCS foods and should not be stored at room temperature due to illness risks.

**31. A:** Heat sanitization involves heating the surface to at least 171 °F and soaking for at least thirty seconds. Choices B, C, and D are incorrect.

**32. A:** Choice A is correct because utensils used to handle raw meat should be washed before handling another type of raw meat. This prevents the spread of bacteria from one type of meat to the other. Choice B is incorrect because sealed meat packaging is not considered a contaminant (only opened packaging is). Choice C is incorrect because placing meat on the bottom shelf appropriately avoids dripping onto other foods. Choice D is incorrect because the employee is wearing gloves.

**33. C:** Choice C is correct because "behavioral design" is one of the seven key areas that the CDC recommends addressing in a policy manual. These key areas are broad, overarching themes rather than specific information. Choices A, B, and D are incorrect because each answer describes specific information rather than a general core topic.

**34. B:** Choice B is correct because process contaminants are chemicals formed during the food preparation process (typically during cooking). As part of the process, they're not typically a contaminant introduced by an employee's poor hygiene. Thus, Choices A, C, and D are incorrect.

**35. B:** Choice B is correct because RTE foods carry the risk of staying too long in the danger zone or having contamination from inappropriately stored raw foods while the RTE food is being stored prior to being set out for the consumer. Choices A, C, and D are incorrect because these steps do not have higher risk than storage.

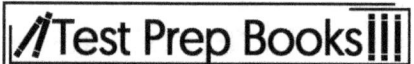

Answer Explanations #3

**36. D:** Choice *D* is correct because hot foods that are being cooled must be reduced to 70 °F or less within two hours of being cooked. Thus, Choices *A* and *B* are incorrect. Choice *C* is incorrect because the ground beef must be cooled to 41 °F after an *additional* four hours—not within four hours of the end of cooking.

**37. A:** MAP stands for modified atmosphere packaging, because the composition of gases (such as oxygen, nitrogen, and carbon dioxide) inside the food packaging are altered to create different atmospheric conditions that reduce food spoilage and the growth of bacteria. Thus, Choice *A* is correct, and Choices *B, C,* and *D* are incorrect.

**38. B:** Choice *B* is correct because the food temperature is a CCP that the CPFM and their employees can address consistently, thereby reducing the risk of foodborne illnesses. Choice *A* is incorrect because the length of shifts does not directly impact food quality (although it may *indirectly* impact quality if workers are tired). Choice *C* is incorrect because the physical layout can help the CPFM identify CCPs in their facility but is not itself a CCP. Choice *D* is incorrect because hazardous waste management is a regulatory requirement but is not part of the food preparation process.

**39. C:** Choice *C* is correct because ready-to-eat hot food may only be served for four hours. Choices *A* and *C* are incorrect because these practices do not increase the risk of foodborne illness. Choice *B* is incorrect because allowing food to cool before refrigeration does not *in general* increase the risk of illness; however, the CPFM must ensure that the food is not allowed to cool for longer than two hours.

**40. C:** Choice *C* is correct because disease-causing bacteria (such as *Salmonella*) typically double in 20 minutes while food is in the danger zone. This is why it's important to promptly ensure that food remains heated or is cooled, even if the food has not yet reached its maximum allowable time ready to serve. Choices *A, B,* and *D* are incorrect.

**41. B:** Ready-to-eat cold food must be kept below 70 °F, so the CPFM must remove the lettuce. Such food must also be removed if it has been out for six hours or longer, so the CPFM must remove the cucumber. The carrots are okay because they have been out for two and a half hours, and their current temperature is below 70 °F. Thus, Choice *B* is correct, and Choices *A, C,* and *D* are incorrect.

**42. D:** Choice *D* is correct because when the air temperature is 90 °F or greater, bacteria is more able to grow and spread, so food must be moved to refrigeration more quickly than the usual two-hour requirement. Choices *A, B,* and *C* are incorrect.

**43. A:** The meal has been in the danger zone for less than two hours, so it is permissible to serve it. The CPFM may also choose to reheat the meal if it is a dish that is best served hot. Thus, Choice *A* is correct, and Choices *B, C,* and *D* are incorrect.

**44. C:** Choice *C* is correct because a steam table is the best device for keeping hot food at a consistent internal temperature of 135 °F or greater. Choice *A* is incorrect because repeatedly microwaving hot food does not consistently keep it out of the danger zone. Choice *B* is incorrect because a heat lamp does not generally provide enough heat to keep food warm for four hours (however, it may be acceptable if the food is provided for less than two hours). Choice *D* is incorrect because the heat of an oven is appropriate for cooking food, not for maintaining heat.

**45. B:** Food should be stirred during the reheating process—especially if using a microwave oven—because this combines the warm and cold parts of the food so that it reaches a consistent safe internal

Answer Explanations #3

temperature. Choice A is incorrect because this is not a safety benefit. Choices C and D are incorrect because the answers are not true.

**46. D:** The acronym "ppm" means "parts per million." It is used to define the quantity of a contaminant that is acceptable in a food product according to the FDA. Thus, Choice D is correct, and Choices A, B, and C are incorrect.

**47. A:** Choice A is correct because the paper wrapping's most important purpose is to reduce the risk of the food becoming contaminated by a member of the public and causing illness in a customer. Choice B is incorrect because the statement is not true. Choice C is incorrect because the nutrition information is a health benefit, not a food safety benefit. Choice D is incorrect because this sanitation benefit does not describe how the wrapper improves the safety of the food *inside* the wrapper.

**48. D:** Choice D is correct because the CPFM should always adhere to the strictest standard when considering food safety, even if a local or federal regulation is less strict. Choices A, B, and C are incorrect.

**49. B:** Choice B is correct because the sliding lid on the trays helps protect the food from pathogens carried in the air. Choice A is incorrect because the trays are open-air. Choice C is incorrect because opening and closing a full freezer to access ice cream provides inappropriate risk that the food will be contaminated through repeated use of the scoop or through the ice cream being left outside the freezer. Choice D is incorrect because there is no method keeping the salad ingredients cool (such as setting the bins in ice).

**50. B:** Choice B is correct because mice get most of their water through the food they eat (such as fruit or meat). Choices A, C, and D are incorrect because cockroaches and rats both typically require a source of standing water to drink. Flies don't have the same requirement for hydration, but do typically seek out standing water for their reproductive cycle.

**51. A:** Choice A is correct because the droppings described best match the droppings of a rat. Choices B and D are incorrect because owls and bats aren't typically associated with food service facilities. Choice C is incorrect because mouse droppings are usually much smaller than a fingernail—small enough to be mistaken for dirt.

**52. D:** Choice D is correct because a mouse's prey instincts discourage it from moving through clear, open spaces. Mowing and weeding the facility's exterior help deter mouse infestations. Choice A is incorrect because cockroaches often enter the building through concealed avenues (such as pipes). Choice B is incorrect because it's unlikely that sparrows or another bird will seek to enter a facility. Choice C is incorrect because clear spaces do not deter flies.

**53. C:** Flies are drawn to garbage as a source of decaying organic material that provides food and water, and also provides a place to lay their eggs. Thus, Choice C is correct. Choices A and B are incorrect because cockroaches and ants are less strongly attracted to garbage than flies. Choice D is incorrect because while raccoons are attracted to garbage, they're not generally considered a pest, as they rarely will try to enter and nest in a facility.

**54. A:** Choice A is correct because rats are known to explore pipes as a means of getting access to buildings and food sources. Choice B is incorrect because, while mice are smaller and better able to squeeze through narrow openings, they're less likely to use methods of travel that may require

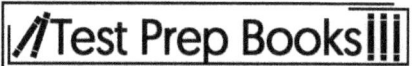

swimming. Choice C is incorrect because ants typically enter a building through ground-floor cracks. Choice D is incorrect because, naturally, flies are able to enter any time a door or window is opened.

**55. B:** The acronym FIFRA stands for the Federal Insecticide, Fungicide, and Rodenticide Act, which the EPA uses to register the use of approved pesticides in the food service industry and other industries. Thus, Choice B is correct, and Choices A, C, and D are incorrect.

**56. A:** Health regulatory authorities require that food service establishments keep records, logs, and forms to demonstrate compliance with the food safety code; therefore, Choice A is correct. While food service establishments keep records pertaining to employee information (Choice B), employee misconduct (Choice C), and their permits and licenses (Choice D), this is not what is meant by the term documentation in this context.

**57. D:** Signage requirements are set by the local health regulatory authority (Choice D). Although the FDA and USDA (Choice C) may provide a framework for the regulations set forth by the local authority, they do not directly set the requirements. Food managers (Choice A) and business owners (Choice B) must comply with the requirements set by the aforementioned authorities.

**58. C:** HACCP plans are put in place to reduce or eliminate the threat of contaminants and pathogens in the food supply by identifying critical control points where contamination is most likely to occur and setting forth requirements to ensure that it does not. While this may indirectly protect employers from lawsuits (Choice A), this is not the purpose of HACCP plans. HACCP plans are not at all related to employee working conditions (Choice B). Although HACCP plans will make an outbreak of foodborne illness less likely, they will do nothing to prevent backlash should one occur (Choice D).

**59. C:** The concept of active managerial control refers to a manager's duty to take proactive control concerning foodborne illness risk factors. Choice B is the only option that pertains to this issue directly. Choices A, C, and D may also be managerial duties, but they are not directly connected with food safety.

**60. A:** The temperature at which bacteria is most likely to thrive is reflected in Choice A as 41°F to 135°F. Refrigeration keeps food below 41°F, and temperatures above 135°F are hot enough to slow bacteria growth substantially.

**61. B:** Choice B is correct because noroviruses and Hepatitis A are the most common viruses causing foodborne illness. Although E. coli is also a common cause of foodborne illness, it is type of bacteria, which renders Choices C and D incorrect. Rhinoviruses are the type of viruses that cause the common cold and are not typically transmitted through food, excluding Choices A and D.

**62. A:** Bivalve molluscan shellfish such as clams and oysters may harbor noroviruses and Hepatitis A due to contamination from feces in the water they grow in. These viruses are capable of surviving cooking temperatures; therefore, these types of fish must be purchased only from approved suppliers.

**63. D:** Wild game and fish are the most likely foods to harbor parasites. To prevent parasitic infection, these foods must be purchased only from approved suppliers and should be cooked and frozen properly.

**64. B:** Exposure to high levels of aflatoxin may lead to death from cancer and liver failure. Although it may cause damage to other organ systems, it is not directly correlated with diabetes, metabolic syndrome, cardiovascular disease, blood clots, lung problems, or esophageal issues.

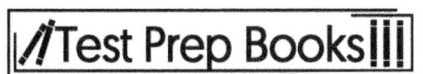

**65. D:** Three of the five leading causes of foodborne illnesses are reflected in Choices A, B, and C. The remaining leading causes of foodborne illness are poor personal hygiene and improper holding times and temperatures. Although Choice D is a potential cause of foodborne illness, it is not one of the top five.

**66. D:** Hepatitis A requires that an employee be removed for a period of thirty days. STEC or shigella only requires a period of three days. Norovirus requires a period of forty-eight hours. Typhoid fever requires a period of fourteen days.

**67. A:** Reportable symptoms include vomiting (Choice A), diarrhea, fever with sore throat, lesions with pus, and jaundice. Although migraines (Choice B), fainting (Choice C), and dizzy spells (Choice D) may be cause for alarm, they are not typically considered risk factors for foodborne illness.

**68. C:** The standard shelf life for refrigerated ready-to-eat TCS foods is seven days, as long as none of their ingredients will expire before this time. If an ingredient will expire before the seven-day period, then the expiration date is the date said ingredient will expire.

**69. C:** Choices A, B, and D all outline approved methods for speeding the cooling of large batches of food. Choice C is incorrect because proofing cabinets are typically used to hold food at temperatures between 70°F and 115°F to create the optimum circumstances for dough to rise, and therefore they are not useful in cooling food to below 41°F.

**70. B:** Foodborne intoxications are illnesses caused by the accumulation of toxins in food via mechanisms such as chemical exposure through fertilizers, pesticides, or cleaning products; improper use of food preservatives; or, as stated in Choice C, naturally occurring toxins that accumulate in seafood. Choices A, B, and D are all causes of foodborne infections, which are foodborne illnesses caused by pathogens.

**71. B:** Choice B is incorrect because an outbreak of foodborne illness is not necessarily the fault of the employees working, and disciplinary action is likely not required. Collecting data from the ill person (Choice A), contacting the local regulatory authority (Choice B), and closing the facility (Choice C) are all actions which may be taken to limit the damage caused by the outbreak and ensure the safety of patrons.

**72. A:** The nine major food allergens include milk, eggs (Choice D), fish (Choice C), shellfish, tree nuts, wheat, peanuts, soybeans (Choice B), and sesame. Choice A, gluten, is not considered one of the nine major food allergens.

**73. D:** Choice D is correct because glassware should never be stacked. Stacking glassware allows it to come into contact with other glasses, which increases the likelihood of breakage due to stress. Also, many units will break if the stack is dropped. Choices A, B, and C all reflect best practices when working with glass.

**74. A:** Ready-to-eat foods should always be stored above raw foods to prevent raw foods from dripping contaminants into the ready-to-eat foods. Choice B is incorrect because foods should be kept below 41°F and above 135°F. Choice C is incorrect because foods should be used first in, first out, so that the oldest food is used before expiration. Choice D is incorrect because raw meat may be stored in the same cooler as produce as long as it is stored beneath.

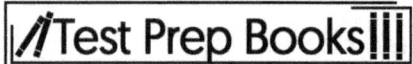

Answer Explanations #3

**75. B:** Cleaning refers to the removal of surface particles, such as dirt, debris, and food particles. Sanitizing refers to the removal of bacteria. Disinfecting refers to the removal of viruses and bacteria. Therefore, Choice *A* is incorrect, and Choice *B* is correct. Choice *C* is incorrect because cleaning only requires soap and water, whereas sanitizing requires specialized chemicals. Choice *D* is incorrect because all chemicals used for cleaning and sanitizing can generally be stored at room temperature.

**76. C:** Food contact areas should be cleaned every four hours during periods of continuous use.

**77. C:** The manufacturer's instructions will give specific information, but generally, sanitizer that contains chlorine should remain on the surface for at least thirty seconds. Choices *A*, *B*, and *D* are incorrect.

**78. D:** Choice *A* is incorrect because chemical sanitation does not require submersion; spraying or otherwise coating a surface works. Choice *B* is incorrect because chemical sanitizers are closely regulated by the EPA, not the FDA. Choice *C* is incorrect because most chemical sanitizers require contact with a surface for a specified period, generally ranging from seven to thirty seconds. Choice *D* is correct because the most common sanitizers include chlorine, iodine, and quaternary ammonium compounds.

**79. C:** Choice *A* is incorrect because the ratio of sanitizer to water matters very much; too little sanitizer can lead to a weak solution that doesn't sanitize properly, while too much can potentially lead to a hazardous solution. Choice *B* is incorrect because the temperature of the water added to the solution can affect how well the sanitizing chemical dissolves. Choice *D* is incorrect because water hardness and pH can also affect the effectiveness of the solution. Choice *C* is correct because color is not necessarily an indicator of the effectiveness of a sanitary solution.

**80. A:** According to manufacturer instructions, machines such as those that hold ice cream and soda should be cleaned every day, typically by running a cleaning or sanitizing solution through the machine.

Dear CPFM Test Taker,

Thank you for purchasing this study guide for your CPFM exam. We hope that we exceeded your expectations.

Our goal in creating this study guide was to cover all of the topics that you will see on the test. We also strove to make our practice questions as similar as possible to what you will encounter on test day. With that being said, if you found something that you feel was not up to your standards, please send us an email and let us know.

We have study guides in a wide variety of fields. If the one you are looking for isn't listed above, then try searching for it on Amazon or send us an email.


Thanks Again and Happy Testing!
Product Development Team
info@studyguideteam.com

# FREE Test Taking Tips Video/DVD Offer

To better serve you, we created videos covering test taking tips that we want to give you for FREE. **These videos cover world-class tips that will help you succeed on your test.**

We just ask that you send us feedback about this product. Please let us know what you thought about it—whether good, bad, or indifferent.

To get your **FREE videos**, you can use the QR code below or email freevideos@studyguideteam.com with "Free Videos" in the subject line and the following information in the body of the email:

    a. The title of your product

    b. Your product rating on a scale of 1-5, with 5 being the highest

    c. Your feedback about the product

If you have any questions or concerns, please don't hesitate to contact us at info@studyguideteam.com.

Thank you!

www.ingramcontent.com/pod-product-compliance
Lightning Source LLC
Chambersburg PA
CBHW080922170426
43201CB00016B/2243